SCIENCE YEAR 9

Published for the Nuffield–Chelsea Curriculum Trust
by Longman Group UK Limited

General Editor
Geoffrey Dorling

Editors
Jacqueline Bradley
Geoffrey Dorling
Andrew Hunt

Authors
David Barlex
Jacqueline Bradley
C. A. Butlin
Harry Cracklow
Geoffrey Dorling
Mark Ellse
Laurence Hall
Patrick Hazlewood
Andrew Hunt
Marian Leftley
David McKnight
Keith Moseley
Philip Poole
Diana Smith
E. J. Wenham
Mary Whitehouse
William H. Yoxall

Advisers
T. P. Borrows
John Groves
Lynda Homer
David Knott
Roger Norris
Alastair Sandiforth
Linda Scott

Longman Group UK Limited
Longman House, Burnt Mill, Harlow, Essex, CM20 2JE, England
and Associated Companies throughout the World.

Copyright © The Nuffield—Chelsea Curriculum Trust 1990

First published 1990
Second impression 1990
ISBN 0 582 01792 0

Set in Monotype Lasercomp 11/14 pt Times New Roman
Produced by Longman Group (FE) Ltd
Printed in Hong Kong

Illustrations by Peter Edwards, Hardlines, John Jamieson and Mark Peppé

Contents

Topic A Materials in the world around us

A1 Resources for chemistry

Our lives would be very different without chemistry. The photograph in figure 1 reminds you of the wide range of chemical products that we use in our homes.

   Very few chemicals are dug up and put straight into bottles. Nearly all of them are manufactured by the chemical industry – from the sea, from the air, from plants and from rocks, as well as from coal and oil.

Figure 1
Search this picture to find examples of each of the following: products for cleaning; materials for making and colouring clothes; drugs and medicines; energy sources; ingredients for processing food; materials for decorating our homes; containers for cooking and eating. Make a list of the examples you find.

One planet

The Earth's resources are not unlimited. As the population grows, it is no longer possible for industry and agriculture to operate without thinking about their effects on the environment. We cannot continue as if it will always be easy to find the fuels, minerals and other resources we like to be able to use. We can only enjoy clean air and pure water if we take care to limit the wastes that are produced on a huge scale by the industries which make the products we hope to buy.

You may hear people talking about 'sustainable development'. Achieving this means finding technologies that are able to provide us with food, warmth, shelter and transport without frittering away limited resources or destroying the natural habitats of plants and animals.

Figure 2
Soil is a vital resource but it forms very slowly and can be quickly washed away. Cutting down trees has caused the soil erosion shown in this picture, taken near Lake Bogoria in Kenya.

Figure 3
These Kenyan students are making barriers to try to stop soil erosion.

Figure 4
This vast hole in the ground is a copper mine near Silver City, USA.

Figure 5
Rubbish at the Everest base camp in Nepal. On average, each home in Britain produces one tonne of rubbish a year. Why don't we do more to recycle the glass, plastic and paper that we throw away so carelessly?

A2 Where chemicals come from

Figure 1
The orange vapour in these pipes is bromine. The pipes are part of chemical equipment for **extracting** bromine from sea water in Anglesey.

Chemicals from the sea

Some people like to cook with sea salt – you can see some in figure 1 on page 2. The sea is also the source of magnesium metal and a liquid called bromine. Bromine itself is dangerous: it burns the skin and gives off choking fumes. But it can be turned into other chemicals needed for photographic film, drugs, fire retardants and **synthetic** rubber.

Chemicals from the air

About one-fifth of the air is a **reactive** gas called oxygen. Oxygen is used to help patients in hospital who are having difficulty with breathing (see figure 2). It is also used to turn iron into steel by burning away **impurities**.

About four-fifths of the air is nitrogen. Liquid nitrogen is useful because it is very cold (see figure 3).

The air also contains small traces of a family of gases that includes helium, neon and argon. These gases are valuable because they are very **unreactive**.

Figure 2
This patient has had a heart attack. He is being given oxygen through a mask to help him breathe.

Figure 3
These pizzas have been fast-frozen by a spray of liquid nitrogen.

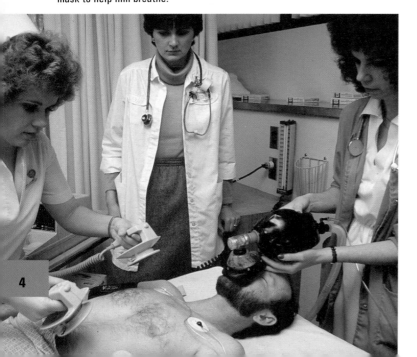

Chemicals from plants

Plants were an important source of **fuel**, building materials, food, clothing, **dyes** and perfumes long before the modern chemical industry came about. We still rely on plants for products that we cannot easily make for ourselves.

Our sugar comes from sugar beet or sugar cane. For thousands of years, **fermentation** has been used to convert plant sugars into alcohol and carbon dioxide.

Figure 4
Sunflower seeds contain an oil which is used to make margarine, cooking oil and soap.

Figure 5
Harvesting lavender in Norfolk for making perfume.

Figure 6
Glass is made by melting pure sand with limestone and other minerals in a furnace. Dollops of the molten glass can be removed from the furnace and blown into shape by craftsmen.

Chemicals from rocks

We get most of our metals from rocks. A rock that is a source of metals is called an **ore**. Rocks are also used as building materials and to make glass (see figure 6). In Britain, huge amounts of limestone are quarried for the chemical industry, for making steel and glass, and to build roads.

Figure 7
Hermann Staudinger and his wife, at work in their home. He was professor of chemistry at Freiburg University in Germany and his theories explained how chemicals from coal and oil could be turned into plastics. He won the Nobel prize in 1953.

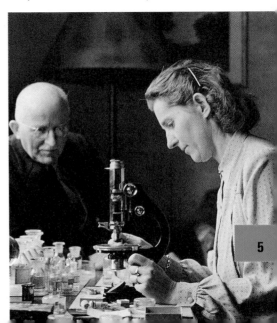

Chemicals from coal and oil

Oil is perhaps the most important source of chemicals at the moment. When the oil runs out we shall have to rely on coal instead. Oil and coal can be used to make fuels, plastics, **fibres**, dyes, farm chemicals and medicines.

On these two pages there are ten words printed in **bold** type. Write down the meanings of these words.

5

A3 Solids, liquids and gases

Figure 1

When you pour a liquid it takes up the shape of the bottle or glass but, just like a solid it has a definite volume and is very difficult to squash

A gas spreads out to fill whatever you put it in

A solid is rigid and keeps its shape. It has a definite volume and is very difficult to squash

It has no definite volume and it's easy to squash

What are scientific theories? Where do they come from? In this unit you have a chance to think about these questions and to explore a very important theory.

Scientists use their imagination to think up theories. The theories may often seem strange at first, so you have to ask yourself, 'What is this strange theory trying to explain?' We shall take the theory used to explain what we know about solids, liquids and gases as an example.

You can see patterns if you look at solids, liquids and gases. Figure 1 shows the patterns that some boys and girls noticed.

How can we explain these observations? There is a theory to answer this question. But you can only make sense of the theory if you use your imagination and build up a picture in your mind of a world made up of minute particles which are much too small to see.

A teacher explains the idea in figure 2.

Figure 2

All solids, liquids and gases are made of very, very tiny pieces called PARTICLES. A single particle is so tiny that you just can't see it, even with the most powerful microscope. The particles are much smaller than grains of sand or specks of dust

For the moment, let's think of these particles as small units such as these. We can explain the way solids, liquids and gases work by using pictures like those in figure 3 to show how the particles are arranged and how they move.

You would need ten million (10,000,000) of these particles to make a line one millimetre (one mm) long

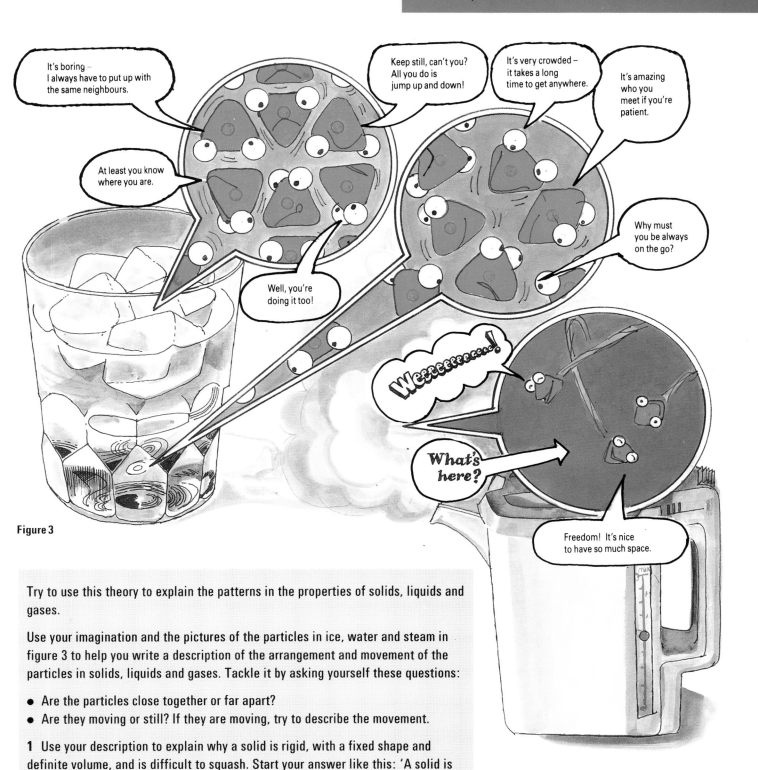

Figure 3

Try to use this theory to explain the patterns in the properties of solids, liquids and gases.

Use your imagination and the pictures of the particles in ice, water and steam in figure 3 to help you write a description of the arrangement and movement of the particles in solids, liquids and gases. Tackle it by asking yourself these questions:

- Are the particles close together or far apart?
- Are they moving or still? If they are moving, try to describe the movement.

1 Use your description to explain why a solid is rigid, with a fixed shape and definite volume, and is difficult to squash. Start your answer like this: 'A solid is rigid because the particles making up a solid are . . .'

2 Use your description to explain why a liquid takes up the shape of its container but still has a definite volume and is difficult to squash.

3 Use your description to explain why gases spread out and are easy to squash.

A4 Dissolving and diffusion

1 Imagine you are a particle in a crystal of coloured dye. You'd be surrounded by other particles of dye – on all sides, and above and below.

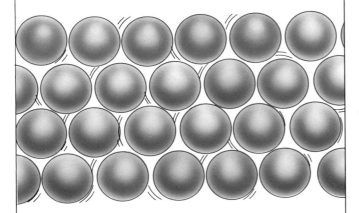

Now, what are you doing, all squashed together? Just jumping about on the spot, really. Scientists call it **vibrating**. You don't go anywhere – you and your friends stay in fixed positions.

2 Now imagine that you are at the edge of the dye crystal. What will you see then? Well, there will be other dye particles all around you, except out in front. There, you'll see air particles whizzing about and crashing into you and your friends. As you don't react with the air, these particles just bounce off.

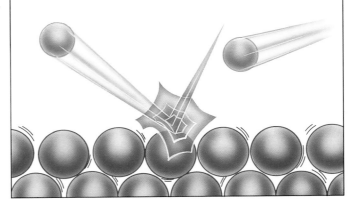

3 But what if your crystal is put in some water? What will you see then? Before you can answer this, you need to imagine what it's like being a particle in liquid water. Well, you'd be completely surrounded by other water particles. But, unlike the particles in the crystal, you'd be doing more than just vibrating. As the water is liquid, you and your friends would be tumbling over each other.

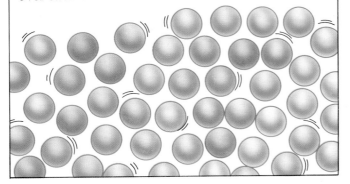

4 So what will happen when the rough-and-tumble crowd of water particles meets the vibrating pack of dye particles? We know that the dye dissolves in the water because the dye colour spreads out from the crystal into the water:

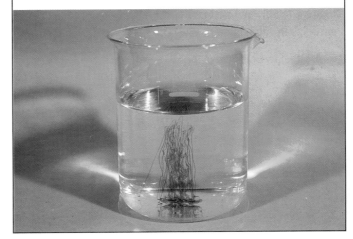

5 But what are the particles doing to cause this to happen? Let's imagine...

6 The water particles are tumbling over each other, so they can press on remorselessly:

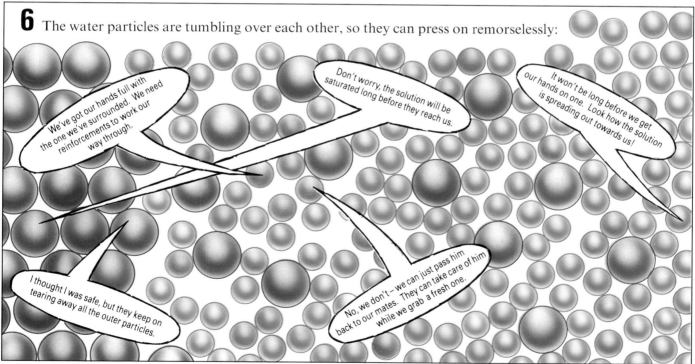

Now try some imaginative writing. Write the story of the dissolving dye from the point of view of the water particles or the dye particles. Your story should try to explain why the dye dissolves, why the dye colour spreads out unaided, and why the colour gets paler further away from the dye crystal.

HOW BIG'S BIG AND HOW SMALL'S SMALL?

Topic **B** **Living earth**

B1 Where does soil come from?

Figure 1
Flowing water has cut this deep canyon.

Figure 2
New land formed at the mouth of the river Nile.

Figure 3
Glaciers like this were once responsible for forming much of the soil over Britain.

Figure 4
Frost-shattered rocks on South Georgia.

Where does soil come from? What do you see if you look at some soil under a microscope? If you look carefully, you will see that there are lots of particles, many of which look like small bits of rock. Mixed in with these you may see plant and animal fragments.

But where do the rocky particles come from? Maybe they were once part of larger rocks. In this unit we shall look at the ways in which rocks can be broken up into small particles.

Water and ice

In Unit E5 you can read about the way water wears away the land. This is a slow process but its effect can be seen all over the world in the form of canyons, gorges and valleys with rivers at the bottom (see figure 1). Small particles of rock are carried away by the river and are later dropped where its flow is slower. This process is called **sedimentation**. Sediments deposited in this way can build up, and eventually form soil. This happens particularly at the mouths of rivers, where new land can be formed (see figure 2). The process of soil formation is very slow – it may take between 100 and 1000 years to build up a layer of new soil 1 cm thick.

Glaciers and ice-sheets also move over rocks and grind them up into small particles (see figure 3). Much of northern Europe was covered by ice in the Ice Ages, which lasted until about 15 000 years ago. When the ice melted, the fine particles of rock were left behind to form soil. A lot of the soil in Britain was formed like this. Ice also breaks up rock in another way. If any water is caught in a crack in the rock and it freezes and expands, the crack will widen. Eventually the rock will break apart (see figure 4).

Chemicals and plants help the process along

Water can also attack some rocks chemically. Rain dissolves some of the carbon dioxide produced by plants and animals. This forms a very weak acid which attacks rocks such as chalk and limestone. The limestone 'pavement' scenery shown in figure 5 is the result of such chemical action.

Plants also help to break up rocks. Their roots can exert very large forces when they grow. This is quite a rapid method of breaking up rock – think how quickly the surface of a little-used road can be damaged by weeds growing up through it (see figure 6).

Figure 5
Limestone 'pavement' scenery in Yorkshire.

Figure 6
Plant life soon starts to break up the surface of a little-used road.

1 Why should trees be planted some distance away from houses?

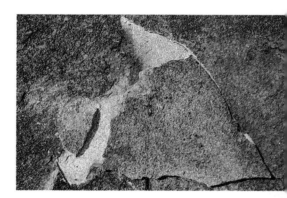

Figure 7
Layers of this rock are flaking off because of changes in the temperature.

Changing temperatures

Changes in temperature can cause rocks to expand and contract. This repeated movement can cause the surface to break off in layers. The rock surface can look rather like an onion peeling (see figure 7).

Figure 8
Volcanoes pour out ash that may eventually form soil. The eruption of Mount St Helen's in the USA in 1980 deposited huge amounts of ash.

Wind

Wind plays only a small part in the breakdown of rocks. Soil particles already formed may be blown against rock and act like a sand-blaster, wearing it away. Wind has a greater effect in spreading soil to different areas once it has been formed. In many areas of the country, hedgerows have been removed from around fields, leaving them exposed to the wind. Many people are concerned about the way wind can blow the top-soil off fields if they are left exposed in this way.

2 What advantages might a farmer gain by removing the hedges around fields?

13

B2 The process continues ...

Figure 1

a Heathers grow on acid soils.

b Milkwort prefers alkaline conditions.

Soil is much more than the rocky particles which form a part of it. Such a material would not support most living things for long! What do plants need from the soil in order to grow?

Firstly, they need water and oxygen, not only in the air around them but also in the soil – oxygen is necessary for good root growth, for example. Secondly, they need a number of other substances that are important for their well-being. These substances are called **plant nutrients**. The part of the soil that helps provide these is called the **humus**. It is formed from plant and animal debris that accumulates and rots in the soil.

You can see in Unit B3 that soils can differ from one another in many ways. Different soils make good homes for different kinds of plants. One way that soils can differ is in whether they are acid or alkaline (see Unit D8). Some plants, such as heathers, need an acid soil to live well, while others, such as milkwort, only live on alkaline soils (see figure 1).

Soil can be made free of life (sterile) by such activities as burning. But even if soil particles start off with no living things growing between them, it is not long before life develops there. This arrival of living things is called **colonization**.

In 1963 a new volcanically-formed island, named Surtsey, appeared off Iceland (see figure 2a). Soil on new land such as this has no life in it. Yet within about twenty years colonization had taken place and plant growth had started (see figure 2b).

1 There are many areas of the world where vegetation is regularly destroyed by fire – either naturally occurring or man-made. Give one or two examples of places where this happens.

Figure 2
a The island of Surtsey which was formed off Iceland in 1964.

b By 1979, the new land had been colonized by plants.

14

In the process of colonization, the first-comers are usually plants called **lichens** (see figure 3). These plants can even gain a foothold on bare rock. When they die, their remains form a soil in which mosses, then ferns, and finally flowering plants can grow. The remains of all these plants form humus. The humus releases plant nutrients and its acidity helps to break up the rock. So the soil changes with time as more rock is broken up and more humus is added. Because of this, the plants that will grow in the soil also change. The next plants to appear are often grasses, followed by other flowering plants, then shrubs, and finally trees (see figure 4). This series of changes is called a **succession**.

In parts of Britain, sand deposits from the sea build up on the coasts as dunes and spits. They are bare of life to start with, but plants soon colonize them. One of the most successful plants at colonizing bare sand is marram grass (see figure 5). These plants have very deep roots which bind the sand particles together.

It is possible to change the nature of a soil to encourage particular plants to grow. For example, potatoes grow best on an acid soil, while cabbages prefer alkaline conditions. Farmers and gardeners are changing the nature of the soil when they add lime to a soil or put in drainage ditches (see figure 6). Adding lime to a clay soil improves the drainage and also makes the soil more alkaline. Interfering with the nature of a soil has to be done with care, as it can cause problems (see Unit B7).

Figure 3
Lichens can even grow on bare rock.

Figure 4
This mature oak wood could represent the last stage in a succession.

2 What other ways are there for farmers to control which plants grow in a field and which do not? Do these methods bring other problems in their wake?

All the processes you have met in this unit and in Unit B1, which act together to break up rock, are known as **weathering**. They can be grouped under three headings:

- Physical weathering
- Chemical weathering
- Biological weathering

Figure 5
Marram grass growing on sand dunes.

Figure 6
A drainage ditch.

3 Draw up a table with these headings:

Physical weathering	Chemical weathering	Biological weathering

Make a list of all the processes that can break up rock, putting each one in the correct column.

B3 A place to live?

Figure 1
Feeling the texture of a soil.

Particle name	Particle size
Gravel	greater than 2 mm
Coarse sand	2 mm to 0.2 mm
Fine sand	0.2 mm to 0.05 mm
Silt	0.05 mm to 0.002 mm
Clay	less than 0.002 mm

Figure 2
Particle sizes in soils.

Soil type	Proportions of the different-sized particles		
	Sand	Silt	Clay
Sandy	more than 80%		
Silty		more than 50%	less than 40%
Loamy	less than 80%	less than 50%	less than 40%
Clayey			more than 40%

Figure 3
Classifying soils by texture.

Are all soils alike? Farmers and gardeners often test soil by picking it up and feeling it (see figure 1). If you try this, you will soon realize that there are many different types of soil. Some are crumbly, containing mainly coarse particles. At the other extreme, some are made of fine particles and become very 'sticky' in wet weather. These differences in the appearance and 'feel' of a soil are described as different **textures**. The texture of a soil depends upon the size of the rock particles in it.

Putting soils into groups

Sorting things into groups is called **classification**. It is useful to classify soils because, as you will see later in this unit, the nature of a soil has a lot to do with what plants will grow on it. Scientists, including the Russian soil scientist V. V. Dokuchaiev, started classifying soils as long ago as 1870. There is more than one way of classifying soils. One way is to describe how acid or alkaline a soil is (see Unit B2). Using soil texture is another way. You may have tried classifying soils for yourself in this way, using a key, in Activity B5.

The particles of rock in soil can be grouped according to their size. The names of the different 'size' groups are shown in figure 2.

Soils often contain particles from more than one of these 'size' groups. Different soil types contain different proportions of the groups, mixed as shown in figure 3.

A soil's particle size determines the quantities of air and water that it will hold. The larger the proportion of small particles, the more water and the less air it will hold. Why do you think this is? Which soil type do you think farmers and gardeners prefer?

Soil profiles

If you look at the sides of a newly-made cutting for a road or a railway, you will notice that the soil seems to be in layers (see figure 4). The series of layers is called a **soil profile**. You can also see soil profiles in other places, such as cliffs and quarries.

1 Builders and construction engineers are often interested in soil profiles. Can you suggest a reason why?

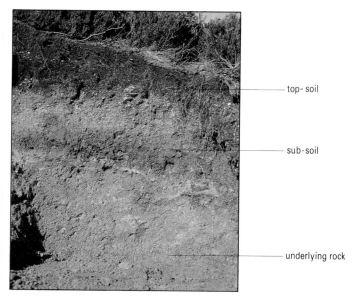

Figure 4
A soil profile exposed by a railway cutting.

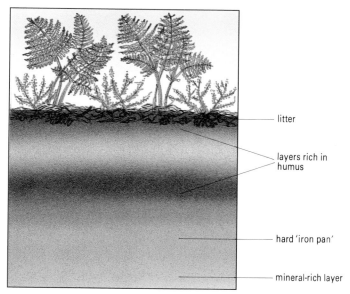

Figure 5
A soil type called a 'podzol'. This soil type is determined partly by the underlying rock and partly by the plants growing on it.

A soil profile shows the top-soil, in which most plants grow, the less fertile sub-soil below it, and finally the rock underneath the soil. This rock is not always the one the soil on top came from. The soil might have been moved there from somewhere else.

2 What might cause a soil to move, so that it no longer lies over its parent rock?

The rock below the soil can determine how well the soil drains. The depth of soil and hardness of the rock beneath may affect the rooting of plants. So the look of the landscape depends partly on the underlying soil profile.

The environment

You have already seen that the plants that will grow on one type of soil are different from the plants that will grow on another. But the soil type is not the only thing that determines which plants will grow in a particular place. Another important factor is the surroundings – something scientists refer to as the **environment**. The surroundings include the climate (what the weather is like), the amount of shade, the wetness (remember – many plants can live under water!), and so on.

Finally, plants can help to create their own environment and their own soil. Large plants – such as trees – can produce shade, deep layers of rotting leaves or pine needles, large roots, and so on. These things will all affect what other plants can grow alongside them.

Figure 6
Plants growing under water.

17

The number of different plants and animals living on the Earth is huge. Scientists have estimated that in one 40 km² patch of rain forest alone (see figure 1), there may be as many as 1500 different types of flowering plants, 750 types of trees and 400 types of birds. No one has yet counted all the different types of insects, but the number is known to be in the tens of thousands. This is only a small fraction of the total number of different species of plants and animals found on the Earth. Why should there be so many? In this unit we shall look at some of the reasons and see how, despite their variety, plants and animals can be classified into groups.

The area where an animal lives is called its **habitat**. The plants in the habitat provide both shelter and food for many of the animals that live there. Both the soil and the climate affect the type of plants that will grow in a particular area (see Unit B3). Because of the wide variety of soils and climates found on the Earth, there are many different habitats.

The plants found in a particular habitat differ from those found in another because some plants are better suited to one soil or climate than another. In a similar way, the animals found in a particular habitat are the ones that are best suited to live there.

Figure 1
Rain forests are very rich in plant and animal life.

Make a list of five different animals. For each one, write down where it lives and describe one way in which the animal is well suited to its habitat.

Figure 2
How are badgers adapted to their habitat?

Variety

No two plants or animals are exactly the same. Pick any two flowers of the same type, say two buttercups, and study them very carefully. You will always be able to find some differences between them. Despite this, you can see that the plants are sufficiently alike to be given the same name. They are said to belong to the same **species**.

If you look carefully in a particular habitat, you may well find two plants that are very similar, but which obviously do not belong to the same species. On a patch of grassland, for instance, you may find corn marigolds and ox-eye daisies (see figure 3). These two plants obviously have some similarities, although they are not from the same species. In fact, they both belong to a **family** of plants called the Compositae. Putting plants and animals into groups is called **classification**. All the plants or animals in a particular group have something in common.

Figure 3
What similarities can you spot between the corn marigolds (yellow) and the ox-eye daisies (white)?

Different groups can be clustered together into even bigger groups (see figure 4) – just as most of the families that live in, say, Canada can be put into a larger group, called 'Canadians'.

Classifying plants and animals – that is, finding the group in which they belong – is a fascinating process. If you can fit a plant or animal into its correct group, you not only feel a sense of triumph but you also learn something more about it. The way to learn about classification is to try doing it for yourself. Handbooks and charts that help you do this are called **keys**. You may have tried using simple keys in science already.

Figure 4
Classifying plants and animals.

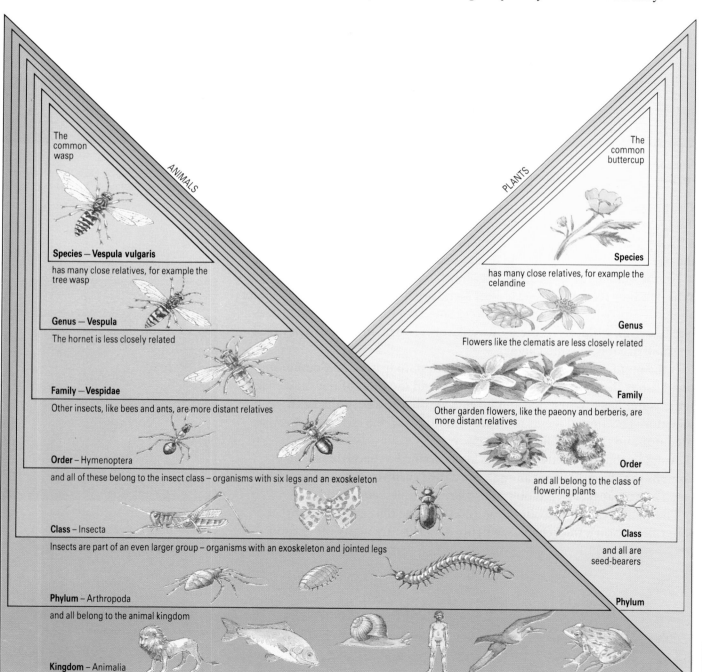

ANIMALS

The common wasp

Species — Vespula vulgaris

has many close relatives, for example the tree wasp

Genus — Vespula

The hornet is less closely related

Family — Vespidae

Other insects, like bees and ants, are more distant relatives

Order – Hymenoptera

and all of these belong to the insect class – organisms with six legs and an exoskeleton

Class – Insecta

Insects are part of an even larger group – organisms with an exoskeleton and jointed legs

Phylum – Arthropoda

and all belong to the animal kingdom

Kingdom – Animalia

PLANTS

The common buttercup

Species

has many close relatives, for example the celandine

Genus

Flowers like the clematis are less closely related

Family

Other garden flowers, like the paeony and berberis, are more distant relatives

Order

and all belong to the class of flowering plants

Class

and all are seed-bearers

Phylum

B5 Food for all

Figure 1
This pond is a habitat for many different living things.

Figure 2
Water fleas. These small animals feed off algae (small organisms) floating in the pond.

The pond shown in figure 1 is a habitat for plants and animals that can live in or on water. If you study a pond closely you will find a great variety of living things there – some of them only visible under a microscope. All the organisms living together in one habitat are called a **community**.

All the animals in this community have to get their food from the pond. What do they feed on? If you collect some pond water and look at it under a microscope you should see some very small creatures called water fleas (see figure 2). Millions of these tiny creatures live in any pond. They feed on small organisms called **algae**.

If the pond is large enough it may also contain fish. A very common pond fish is the stickleback (see figure 3) – and the food of the stickleback is the water fleas. When one animal eats another it is described as a **predator**. The animal it eats is its **prey**. In this case, the stickleback is the predator and the water fleas are its prey.

Animals that feed only on plants are described as **herbivores**, while animals that feed on other animals are called **carnivores**. Some animals (such as humans) can feed on both – they are called **omnivores**.

The sticklebacks, the water fleas and the algae that are food for the water fleas form a **food chain** (see figure 4). There are many other food

Figure 3
These sticklebacks feed off the water fleas.

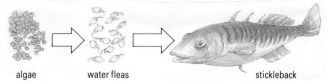

algae   water fleas   stickleback

algae   water fleas   dragonfly larva

Figure 4
A simple food chain.

Figure 5
Another food chain.

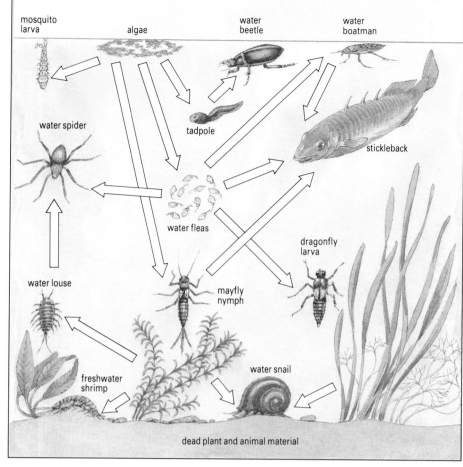

mosquito larva   algae   water beetle   water boatman   water spider   tadpole   stickleback   water fleas   dragonfly larva   water louse   mayfly nymph   freshwater shrimp   water snail   dead plant and animal material

Figure 6
A food web for a pond.

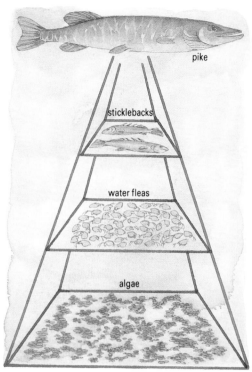

pike   sticklebacks   water fleas   algae

Figure 7
A pyramid of numbers for a food chain in a pond.

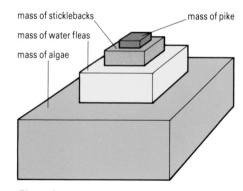

mass of sticklebacks   mass of pike   mass of water fleas   mass of algae

Figure 8
A pyramid of biomass for the same food chain.

chains in a pond, several of them starting with the same algae and the water fleas. Figure 5 shows one of these. These two chains can be put together. The two chains linked together are the start of what is called a **food web** (see figure 6). Food webs show how all the organisms in a habitat are linked to each other in the way they feed. A food web can look quite complicated. For example, not only do water fleas provide the food for several different predators, but any one predator, such as a stickleback, feeds on many other organisms as well as on water fleas.

If the stretch of water which is home to the sticklebacks and the water fleas is the size of a small lake, it may support another predator – the pike. Pike feed off small fish, such as sticklebacks. A pike is a further step along the food chain.

A lake of about 4000 square metres might be able to support just one or two pike. The same lake would contain hundreds of sticklebacks and millions of water fleas. The water fleas in turn will feed off millions and millions of tiny algae.

In this food chain, the number of organisms of a particular type gets smaller and smaller as you pass along the chain. We can show this in a diagram, called a **pyramid of numbers** (see figure 7).

A better way to show this fact is to make a pyramid of the masses of the different organisms in the food chain (see figure 8). This is called a **pyramid of biomass**.

Rose bushes are a habitat for many aphids. The aphids live off the leaves of the bush. Ladybirds will also live on a rose bush. Their food is the aphid population. Draw a food chain and a pyramid of numbers for the rose-bush community. Explain why a pyramid of biomass would make more sense.

B6 Farming the land

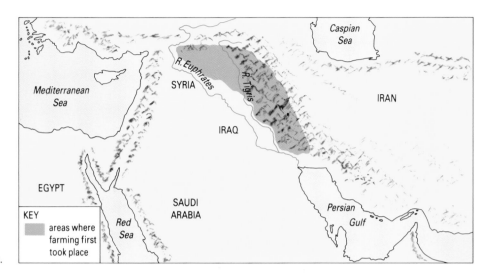

Figure 1
Where it all began.

The soil supports a wide range of plants and animals. We use many of the plants as food. Humans are believed to have started growing plants for food in about 10 000 BC, in the part of the world now called Iraq (see figure 1).

Plants grown for food are called **crops**. Any other unwanted plant, growing among the crops, is called a **weed**. A weed might be a plant from last year's crop, growing among this year's.

The main crops grown in different countries differ from one part of the world to another (see figure 2). This is often because the different soils and the different environments are best suited to different plants.

Figure 2
Main crops throughout the world.

a Millet in Kenya.　　　　b Peanuts in India.　　　　c Potatoes in Ireland.

d Sugar beet in East Anglia.　　　　e Wheat in the USA.　　　　f Rice in the Philippines.

Cultivation

The process of growing plants in soil is called **cultivation**. The same process is used throughout the world, although different tools may be used. Figure 3 shows the important steps a farmer has to take in cultivating crops.

Figure 3
The farming cycle.

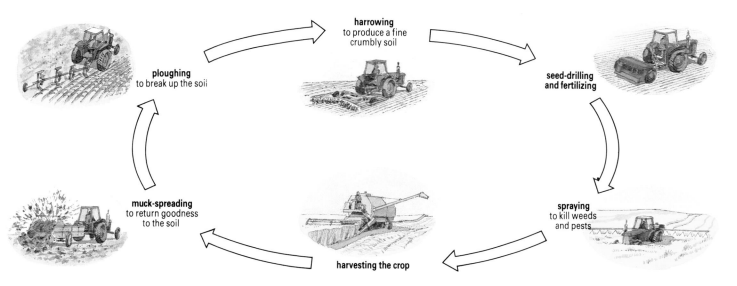

ploughing
to break up the soil

harrowing
to produce a fine
crumbly soil

seed-drilling
and fertilizing

spraying
to kill weeds
and pests

harvesting the crop

muck-spreading
to return goodness
to the soil

Getting help from the worms

Many animals live in the soil, but one animal in particular helps the process of cultivation. That animal is the worm. There may be as many as 13 million worms living in an area of one square kilometre. The worms' activity in the soil helps to mix up soil layers. Worms also help by pulling dead plant materials from the surface into the soil, so increasing its humus content. Worms live in burrows in the soil. The burrows allow air into the soil and help drainage. While it is burrowing through the soil, a worm takes in soil particles and dead plant material to use as food. Once this material has passed through the worm's body, it forms a sticky mixture of soil particles. This often appears on the surface and is then called a 'worm cast'. Worm casts are ideal for seed growth. Worms give a fine texture to the soil without using any machinery!

Worms take nothing out of the soil that is not eventually returned to it, so the soil remains good and fertile. Farmers take a great deal from the soil when they harvest crops. They have to be careful to see that the soil gets back what it loses to one year's crops if cultivation is to continue.

In many countries, farmers can produce enough crops for them to be able to sell them to other people (see figure 4). In other parts of the world, farmers may still not be able to produce enough food to feed even their immediate families (see figure 5).

Figure 4
Farming in an area of rich soil.

Figure 5
Subsistence farming on poor soil in Brazil.

23

We use the soil to grow our food. To do this, land areas are cleared and steps are taken to increase crop yields. It is essential to use fertilizers – natural, artificial, or both. Weeds and pests have to be controlled. Farmers also make use of machinery to help in cultivation and harvesting.

All these things have improved food production but, without careful use, they can bring problems in their wake. We shall look at some of these problems in this unit.

Using farm machinery

Farm machinery, such as ploughs and harvesters, is essential to modern farming (see figure 2). To accommodate large modern machines, fields have been enlarged by removing hedges. This exposes the soil to the full force of the wind. If the soil is light, it may dry out. The next wind that comes along may blow away the top, dry layer of fertile soil, leaving only the unproductive sub-soil below (see figure 3).

Figure 1
Intensive cultivation of bananas and olives in Israel.

Figure 2
Using farm machinery in Canada.

Figure 3
A sandstorm in the UK.

Figure 4
Using farmyard manure can help to maintain the soil's structure.

The **structure** of a soil is the way the rocky particles are joined together. A crumbly structure is ideal for plants. Without care, continued use of heavy machinery may destroy the soil's structure. The soil is compressed and, although the surface layer can be broken up by ploughing, the lower layers may gradually form a hard sheet called a **pan**. This prevents the soil from draining properly and stops air getting into it.

Using fertilizers

Soil fertility can be improved by the use of both chemical and 'organic' fertilizers (such as farmyard manure). But soil needs a good structure as well as the right nutrients if plants are to grow well. Humus sticks soil particles together and helps to give this good structure. If artificial fertilizers are used exclusively, the soil structure may be damaged because its humus content is not maintained. This has already happened in parts of America and Western Europe.

Using too large a quantity of any fertilizer (whether artificial or natural) can mean that unused chemicals are washed out of fields and into ditches and rivers. This may give rise to a number of unwanted effects, such as the algal 'bloom' shown in figure 5.

Controlling weeds and pests

A healthy soil is usually the home for many different types of plants and animals, all helping each other. Chemical compounds that control weeds and pests have to be used with care. They may upset the balance of plants and animals in an unexpected way. They can also reach plants and animals for which they were not intended.

The effect on the rain forests

In tropical areas, the natural vegetation is rain forest. This forest is home to a very large number of species of plants and animals. It also helps to maintain the oxygen level in the Earth's atmosphere.

In many areas of the world, the rain forest is being cut down to gain both land for crops and timber from the trees. The soil that is left does not support food crops for very long. It is eroded away by the weather and the land becomes barren (see figure 6). The forest does not re-grow.

There is a need to maintain and improve the world's food supply. But the soil is the home for many other animals and plants, and both they and the soil can affect our lives in many ways. We also need to use the same soil for growing crops year after year. All these things have to be borne in mind when trying to make the best use of the soil for food production.

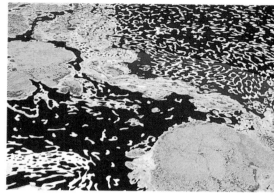
Figure 5
The results of fertilizers entering a stream.

You can read about food chains and food webs in Unit B5. Explain how food chains could lead to a pesticide getting where it was not wanted.

Figure 6
Burning down rain forests may leave behind barren soil, as in this photograph.

Figure 7
Allowing cattle to graze for too long on one piece of land can destroy the soil. Think of some of the reasons why.

25

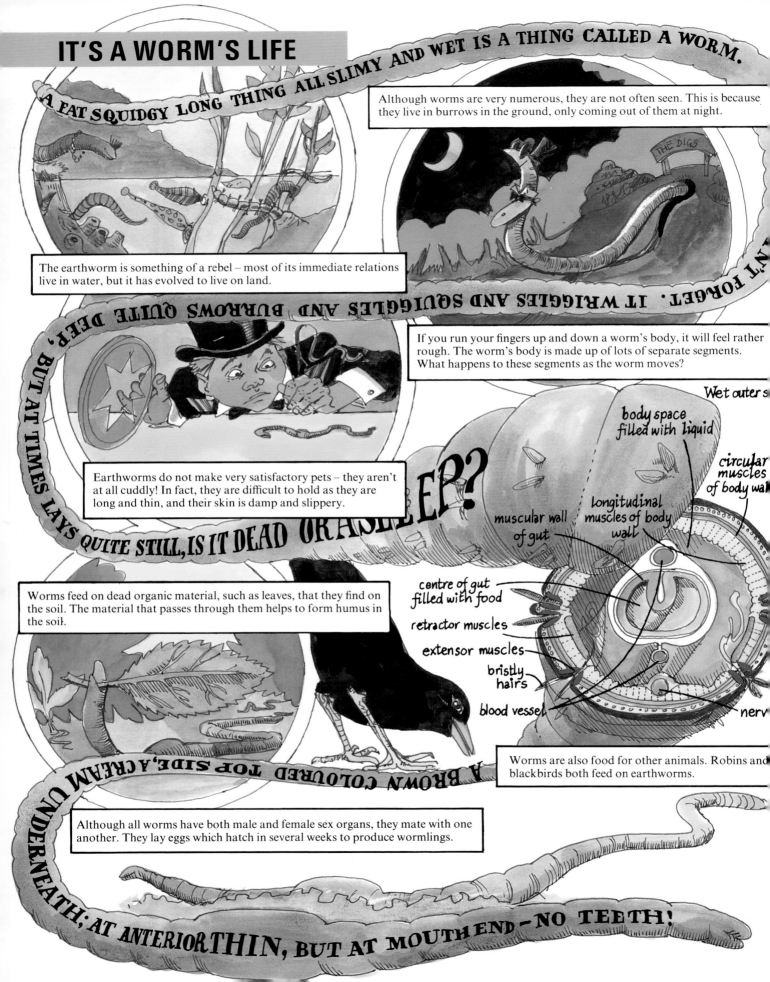

IT'S A WORM'S LIFE

A FAT SQUIDGY LONG THING ALL SLIMY AND WET IS A THING CALLED A WORM.

Although worms are very numerous, they are not often seen. This is because they live in burrows in the ground, only coming out of them at night.

The earthworm is something of a rebel – most of its immediate relations live in water, but it has evolved to live on land.

N'T FORGET. IT WRIGGLES AND SQUIGGLES AND BURROWS QUITE DEEP,

If you run your fingers up and down a worm's body, it will feel rather rough. The worm's body is made up of lots of separate segments. What happens to these segments as the worm moves?

BUT AT TIMES LAYS QUITE STILL, IS IT DEAD OR ASLEEP?

Earthworms do not make very satisfactory pets – they aren't at all cuddly! In fact, they are difficult to hold as they are long and thin, and their skin is damp and slippery.

Worms feed on dead organic material, such as leaves, that they find on the soil. The material that passes through them helps to form humus in the soil.

Worms are also food for other animals. Robins and blackbirds both feed on earthworms.

UNDERNEATH; AT ANTERIOR THIN, BUT AT MOUTH END — NO TEETH!

A BROWN COLOURED TOP SIDE, A CREAM

Although all worms have both male and female sex organs, they mate with one another. They lay eggs which hatch in several weeks to produce wormlings.

Wet outer s

body space filled with liquid

circular muscles of body wall

muscular wall of gut

longitudinal muscles of body wall

centre of gut filled with food

retractor muscles

extensor muscles

bristly hairs

blood vessel

nerv

Topic **C** **Energy**

C1 Talking about energy

Figure 1

Figure 2
The sails of this windmill are moving. Suggest three useful tasks that the windmill might do.

This is natural milk. Average butterfat content 3.8% AVERAGE CONTENTS PER 100 ml	
KILOCALORIES	65
(KILOJOULES	280)
PROTEIN	3.4 g
FAT	3.8 g
CARBOHYDRATE	4.8 g

Figure 3
Which of this information tells us how much energy we can obtain from the milk?

Figure 4
Some domestic energy-using devices.

Figure 1 shows some of the things some girls and boys said when they were talking about energy. Do you agree with them? It is much easier to talk about the things that energy can or cannot do, than it is to explain what energy is. This topic should help you to understand more about energy and why it is so important to us.

If we say that Gary is a 'kind' boy, it is because we have seen him do something kind. In the same way, if we say that Karen has 'lots of energy', it is perhaps because we see her dashing around everywhere. We know that something has energy because it can use that energy to make something happen.

We get energy from many different sources to do work for us. Often we can use the same source of energy to do many different tasks.

1 Make a list of as many sources of energy as you can think of.

Sometimes we can choose one of several different ways of doing a particular task. Then we have to decide which way would be the best. We have to think about the cost, the convenience, how much energy is needed and how much is available.

When we have to make decisions like this, it would help if we could *measure* how much energy a particular task needs. Engineers have to make this sort of decision when they decide how big a motor to put in a washing machine, or whether they can make a computer that will run from a torch battery.

Figure 5
The heavier the bricks, the more energy is needed.

Figure 6
The higher the bricks have to be lifted, the more energy is needed.

Here is one way to measure the energy needed for a particular task. Suppose a 'brickie' has to carry some bricks up a building (see figures 5 and 6). We say that 'The energy used to lift the bricks is given by the weight of the bricks times the vertical height the bricks are lifted'. In general, for any force-using task,

$$\begin{array}{c} \text{energy} \\ \text{needed} \end{array} = \begin{array}{c} \text{force} \\ \text{used} \end{array} \times \begin{array}{c} \text{distance moved in the} \\ \text{direction the force acts} \end{array}$$

Energy is measured in units called **joules**. James Joule was a famous amateur scientist who lived in the nineteenth century. He spent most of his life measuring energy transfers. There is a story that when he was on his honeymoon he showed that the water at the bottom of a waterfall was warmer than the water at the top. He also made other discoveries, which you will learn about later in your work in science.

The word 'joule' can be shortened to the letter 'J'. In any task like the one lifting the bricks, we find the energy needed (in joules) by measuring the force used (in newtons) and the distance moved (in metres).

Figure 7
James Prescott Joule.

$$\underset{\text{(joules)}}{\begin{array}{c} \text{energy} \\ \text{needed} \end{array}} = \underset{\text{(newtons)}}{\begin{array}{c} \text{force} \\ \text{used} \end{array}} \times \underset{\text{(metres)}}{\begin{array}{c} \text{distance moved in the} \\ \text{direction the force acts} \end{array}}$$

---

2 How much energy would be needed to lift some bricks weighing 200 newtons a vertical height of 6 metres?

It is not always so easy as this to work out the energy a task needs. Figure 8 lists the energy values to do some other tasks. For the moment you will have to take them 'on trust'.

Energy-using task	Energy value
Boiling a kettle of water	500 kJ
Travelling 40 km by car	100 kJ
Doing the ironing for an hour	300 kJ
Running upstairs	1.5 kJ
Running a bedside light for an hour	200 kJ

Figure 8
Some energy-using tasks, with their energy values. (1 kJ = 1000 J)

C2 Transferring energy

Have you ever used a stove that runs from a small gas cylinder? Many people use them when they go camping or caravanning. A gas stove uses energy. It gets this energy from the gas, by burning it. But the stove does not stay alight for ever. After a time, it goes out and you find that the gas cylinder is empty. The energy the stove gave out has been obtained from the gas which was once in the cylinder.

If you investigate any energy-using task you will find that the energy used has to be obtained from something else. The energy gained by one thing is lost by another. We cannot make energy. We have to get it from somewhere. So, instead of talking about *using* energy, we find it more helpful to talk about *transferring* energy. This reminds us that the energy used for a task is always lost by something else. Often the energy comes from burning a **fuel**, such as the gas in the cylinder of the stove.

Figure 1
Using a gas stove to heat some water.

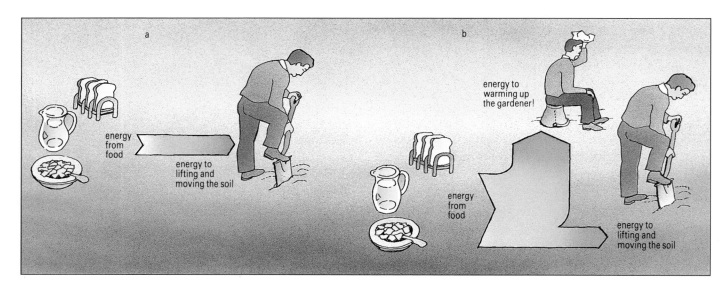

Figure 2

A windmill obtains its energy from the moving air. We obtain our energy from the food we eat. A gardener, digging the garden, is transferring some of the energy stored in his last meal to lifting and moving the soil. The diagram in figure 2a illustrates this energy transfer.

When an energy transfer happens, not all the energy is transferred to doing the things we want. For instance, the gardener will start to feel very hot after digging for some time. The energy diagram can be redrawn to include this 'unwanted' energy transfer as well (see figure 2b).

Figure 3 shows a hydroelectric power station. The pipes bring water from a reservoir up the hill. How do we know that the water stored in the reservoir has energy? Even though we cannot see it doing anything, we

Figure 3
Hydroelectric power station at Loch Lomond.

know that if the dam burst and water was released suddenly, it would do a great deal of damage. When the water is released, gravity pulls it down the hill. At the bottom, electric generators transfer the energy from the water to electricity. The electricity then transmits the energy to the homes and factories where it is needed.

Energy is also stored in fuels such as oil, coal and gas. The energy is transferred from the fuels by burning them, when a chemical reaction takes place.

Energy can also be stored by changing the shape of something. For instance the dynamo in figure 4 can be driven for a short time using energy originally stored in the spring.

Figure 4
A spring-driven dynamo.

When a rubber band is stretched, energy is stored in it. Describe a device which uses a rubber band to make something move.

The energy stored in moving objects

Have you ever been down a helter-skelter? First of all you have to climb up some stairs to the top. To do this you use up some of the energy from your last meal to lift yourself up against the pull of the Earth's gravity. You gain energy because you are higher up than you were at the start.

As you slide down the helter-skelter, what happens to this energy you have gained? You go faster and faster until you reach the ground again! The longer the slide, the faster you travel. Some of the energy you gained in climbing to the top of the helter-skelter is used to increase the speed at which you slide down. Some more of it is used to push you against the friction between you and the slide. The diagram in figure 6 shows the energy transfers. On a very long slide, you may reach a steady downward speed. Energy is then no longer being transferred to increase your speed. Instead, all the energy is being used to push you against the friction between you and the slide.

Cars use a lot of energy (stored in petrol) just to keep them moving at a steady speed. The energy is mainly used to push aside the air through which they move. The faster a car moves, the more energy it has to use to push the air aside. This fact is very important to car designers, who want to cut down fuel consumption. They design the cars' shape so that they can move easily through the air.

High fuel consumption is not the only reason for keeping car speeds down. High speeds in the wrong place and at the wrong time can be dangerous as well.

Figure 5
Helter-skelter!

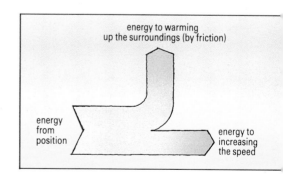

energy to warming up the surroundings (by friction)

energy from position

energy to increasing the speed

Figure 6

Figure 7
A racing driver has to be particularly aware of the dangers of speed.

31

C3 Making life easier

Machines

The farmer shown in figure 1 lives in an area where there is very little rainfall. Water has to be transferred from a nearby river to irrigate the fields. As the farm is a long way from fuel supplies, the farmer has to use his own energy to do this. One way would be to lift buckets of water from the river and empty them into the channels which carry the water to the fields. This would take the farmer far too long, so he uses a machine to help him.

We use many machines every day to help us to do things more easily. Machines can help us in different ways. The pictures in figure 2 show some of them.

Figure 1
Using a 'Persian wheel' for irrigation in Pakistan.

Figure 2
What machines can do.

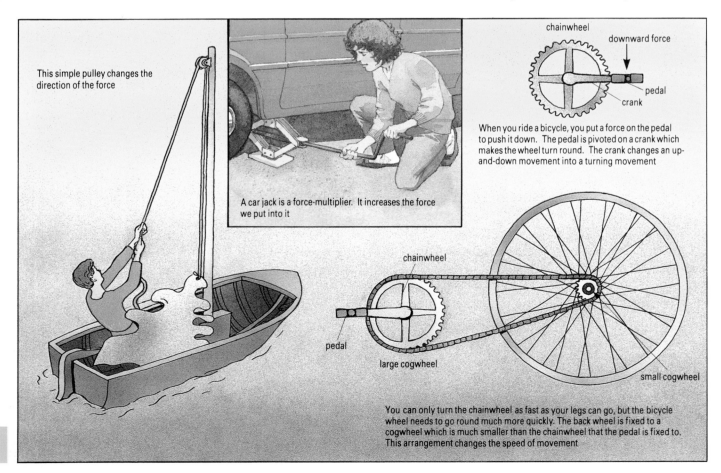

This simple pulley changes the direction of the force

A car jack is a force-multiplier. It increases the force we put into it

When you ride a bicycle, you put a force on the pedal to push it down. The pedal is pivoted on a crank which makes the wheel turn round. The crank changes an up-and-down movement into a turning movement

chainwheel
downward force
pedal
crank

chainwheel
pedal
large cogwheel
small cogwheel

You can only turn the chainwheel as fast as your legs can go, but the bicycle wheel needs to go round much more quickly. The back wheel is fixed to a cogwheel which is much smaller than the chainwheel that the pedal is fixed to. This arrangement changes the speed of movement

Using fuels

People who live in towns and cities throughout the world have come to rely on machines powered by electricity to make life easier for them. An egg-beater turned by hand will do its job perfectly well. But it is much easier to use one driven by an electric motor.

Figure 3
This power station enables energy to be transferred from coal to users by electricity.

Electricity now provides many people with most of their energy needs in the home. It runs hair-driers and toasters, egg-beaters and ovens. It is used for heating. It is the only way to power televisions and radios. Without electricity, there would be no computers, so industry, banks and many other organizations would come to a standstill.

Electricity is an easy way of transferring energy from place to place. Most of the electricity used in Britain comes from large generators driven by steam turbines. The energy to turn the water into steam is supplied by a fuel. A fuel is a very useful energy store — the energy is very concentrated. The table in figure 4 gives the energy content of three fuels that are used in many homes and power stations.

Figure 4
Energy data. (1 MJ = 1 000 000 J)

Fuel	Energy content
Coal	32 MJ per kg
Natural (mains) gas	39 MJ per m^3
Fuel oil	37 MJ per litre

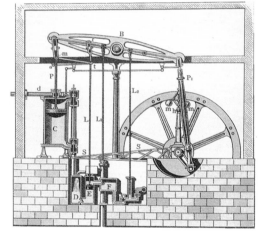

Figure 5
James Watt's steam-driven pumping engine.

Figure 6
Steam locomotive hauling a train.

Engines

Steam engines transfer energy from coal to do work. Years ago there were more of them in use in Britain than there are today. Steam engines were invented to make mining safer and easier. They were used to pump air down coal mines and to pump water out to drain them. Steam engines (locomotives) were regularly used on the railways. Steam engines are not the only way that energy in fuel can be transferred so that we can make use of it. The engines in cars and motorbikes transfer energy from petrol to do the job of moving these vehicles from place to place.

All of these devices which transfer energy from fuels are called **engines**. They, more than anything else, have 'made life easier'.

33

C4 Checks and balances

Figure 1
Drink-vending machine.

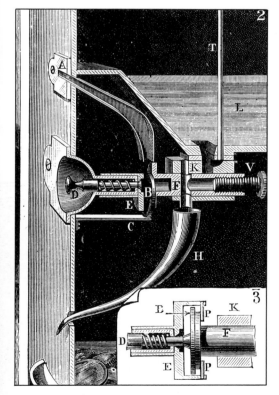

Figure 2
French perfume-vending machine, made in 1893. Can you see how it worked? Part A is the slot for the coin, part B shows the coin already inserted, and part H is the tube down which the perfume flowed.

34

The machines described in Unit C3 all made life easier by changing the force needed to do something or changing the speed. There are other machines that are both useful and convenient, but in a different way. One such device is the slot machine.

Slot machines were invented to sell things without employing someone to do the job. You may have a slot machine that sells drinks in your school, sports centre or youth club. All you have to do is to put your money in the slot and push a button, and the machine will give you your chosen drink. Many modern machines will even give you change if you put in too much money.

Slot machines are not all that new. The first ones were just boxes that could be opened by inserting a coin. They were made in the seventeenth century and contained snuff and tobacco. The earliest slot machines that looked anything like the ones you see today were made in the USA. Many of them were designed to sell chewing-gum.

A coin-operated machine has to do more than simply give goods in exchange for money. The machine has to be able to test whether coins really have been put in the slot! Then it has to be able to tell whether enough money has been paid.

Imagine you are using a simple slot machine that accepts only 10p coins. First the machine checks that the coin is the right diameter and the right thickness.

How would you stop coins of **a** too large a diameter, or **b** too great a thickness, from being used?

If the coin passes the thickness and diameter tests, it still might not be the correct coin to use – or it might not be a coin at all! So the next thing the machine does is to check the coin's weight. The weight of a coin depends not only on its size but also on what metal it is made from. By checking the weight on a balance, the slot machine can reject coins that are the wrong weight, even if they are the right size. Look at the diagram in figure 3 to see how this is done.

Checking the weight

The **weight** of an object is the force of the Earth's gravitational pull on it. Like other forces, weight is measured in **newtons**. The weight of an object depends on its mass – the bigger the mass, the bigger the weight. The **mass**

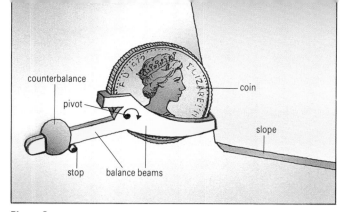

Figure 3
Balance mechanism for checking a coin's weight.

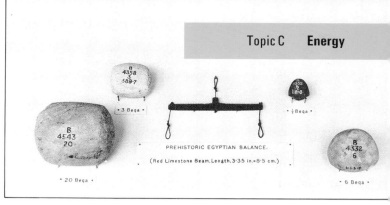

Figure 4
Egyptian balance and stone masses on display in the Science Museum.

of an object tells us how much there is of it. 2 kg of sugar contains twice as much sugar as 1 kg.

Weighing something to find out how much of it there is, is not a new idea. The early Egyptians, 7000 years ago, are known to have used a two-pan equal-arm balance. A red limestone balance has been found in a tomb at Naqada. It is 85 mm long and has stone masses to go with it. Later on, these masses were made in the shapes of animals. The smallest so far discovered has a mass of 6.5 g, and the largest, 60.55 kg. Weighing was used as an aid to collecting taxes, as well as for buying and selling. People who owned land had to pay taxes in kind (goods). Wheat was often used for this. The wheat would be placed in one pan of the balance. Masses were added to the other pan until they balanced the wheat. Because the balance had equal arms, the mass of the wheat was then equal to the masses placed in the other pan.

Some more weighing machines

The Romans introduced the unequal-arm balance, called the 'steelyard'. There is a picture of one in figure 5. The object to be 'weighed' was placed on the right-hand side. The small mass, in the shape of a figure, was then slid along the arm on the left-hand side until it balanced the weight of the object on the right. Markings were put on this arm to show the mass. Steelyards are still used today. You may see one in a butcher's shop, where they are used to weigh whole sides of beef.

A spring balance is a different sort of weighing machine. The stretch of the spring depends on the weight of the mass hung on it. One of the earliest references to the use of a spring balance is found in a book called *The Book of Balance of Wisdom* by al-Khazini, an Islamic physicist. This book was written in the twelfth century AD.

Modern weighing machines are often electronic. A special device inside them (called a **transducer**) converts the force exerted by the object on the scale-pan into an electrical signal. This signal is processed by electronic circuits, and the mass is shown in a window. These machines are often used in greengrocers' shops, where vegetables and fruit are frequently sold by mass. As well as displaying the mass, such machines also calculate the cost of the purchase.

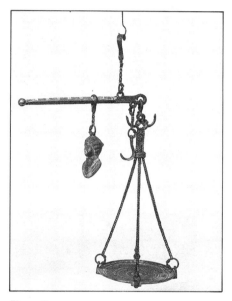

Figure 5
Bronze Roman steelyard, found at Pompeii.

Figure 6
This greengrocer's electronic weighing machine will tell you the cost as well as the mass.

35

C5 From hot to cold

Figure 1
This car engine has got very hot indeed!

One of the things you may have noticed about using energy is that things often get hotter in the process. You get hot if you do a lot of physical activity. Engines and motors all get hotter when they are used. Car engines get so hot that water has to be used to cool them down. It looks as if 'getting hot' is one result of transferring energy. It seems likely that hot things contain more energy than cold ones do.

Energy and the particle model

As you know, we measure the temperature of an object when we want to know how hot it is. Hot objects have high temperatures; cold objects have low temperatures. You have also learned that we believe that all things are made up of particles (see Unit A3). There is evidence that these particles are continually on the move.

Making something like water hotter means transferring energy to it. How might this affect the particles that we believe water is made of? One way is that they could be moving faster.

From liquid to gas

The particles of a liquid are moving, but they are held together in a crowd by forces (see figure 3 on page 7). If energy is transferred to a liquid, the particles move faster. They may get so much energy that they can break away from the force holding them close together. When the particles break free from one another, they spread out into all the space around them. This is what happens when water boils. The liquid water changes to a gas called 'steam'.

This process is one way we can transfer energy from a fuel and make use of it. The fuel is burned and the energy released is transferred to slow-moving particles of water. The water particles pick up this energy and the liquid water turns into a gas with fast-moving particles – steam.

Figure 2
Shaking a tray with a few marbles on it can give you an idea of what a gas is like.

Figure 3
A piston beneath the tube keeps these spheres on the move so that they behave something like a gas.

Transferring energy from a hot gas

When a gas is made hotter and hotter, the particles move faster and faster. If the hot gas is trapped inside a cylinder containing a piston, the fast-moving particles collide with the piston and exert a force on it. The force from the gas moves the piston. So work is being done and energy is transferred from the gas to where it is needed. This is how both steam engines (see figure 4) and car engines work. The force with which a gas presses on its surroundings is its **pressure**. Raising the temperature of a gas in an enclosed space raises its pressure.

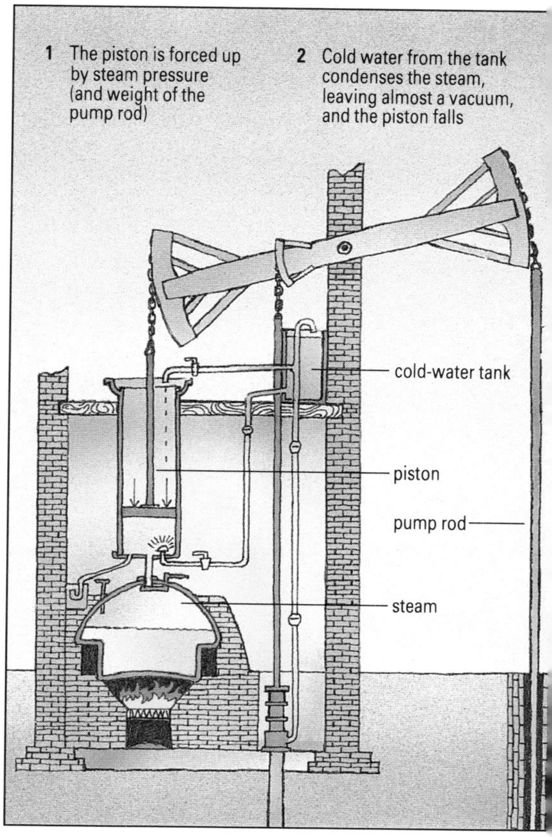

'Losing' energy

Most electricity is generated by burning coal in power stations, but not all the energy from the coal is available as electricity at the output from the power station. Figure 5 shows some of the ways in which the energy is 'lost'.

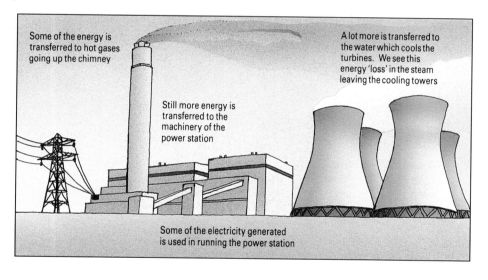

Some of the energy is transferred to hot gases going up the chimney

Still more energy is transferred to the machinery of the power station

A lot more is transferred to the water which cools the turbines. We see this energy 'loss' in the steam leaving the cooling towers

Some of the electricity generated is used in running the power station

Figure 5
'Losing' energy from a power station.

Getting spread out

Although the energy is very concentrated when it is locked up in the fuel, it becomes much less concentrated as soon as we use it. We release the energy from fuels by burning them. As soon as something becomes hotter than its surroundings, it begins to transfer energy to the surroundings.

When energy is transferred to the surroundings, it is spread out among many particles. When energy becomes spread out in this way, it cannot be re-used to do useful tasks.

All the energy we use eventually becomes spread out in the surroundings. Energy cannot be made or destroyed. But when we use a bit of the energy stored in fuels, it is gone for ever, as far as its usefulness is concerned. This is why we are concerned to use all our stocks of stored energy as efficiently as possible.

Figure 4
How Thomas Newcomen's steam engine worked.

1 The piston is forced up by steam pressure (and weight of the pump rod)

2 Cold water from the tank condenses the steam, leaving almost a vacuum, and the piston falls

cold-water tank

piston

pump rod

steam

The cost of electricity in 1988 was approximately 6p per unit (3.6 MJ), of which about 3p paid for the coal used. What other costs are involved in generating electricity?

37

C6 The Earth's energy resources

One of the results of using energy is that it becomes spread out into the surroundings. Once this has happened, it cannot all be used again to do useful tasks. Because of this, we depend on **energy resources** to give us the energy we need.

As we have already seen, one of the most convenient ways of supplying energy to where it is needed is to use electricity. In Britain, most of this electricity is generated by steam turbines.

Figure 1
This coal-fired power station is sited next to the mine which provides its fuel. A convenient arrangement, but what happens when the coal runs out?

Figure 2
Hunterston 'B' nuclear power station at Strathclyde, Scotland.

Figure 3
Victoria hydroelectric power station on the River Mahaweli in Sri Lanka.

Many power stations use coal, oil or (occasionally) gas to change water into high-pressure steam. But these fuels, called **fossil fuels**, will eventually run out. There is also concern about the way that gases from the power stations' chimneys can pollute the environment. Steps are now taken in many power stations to remove harmful substances from the waste gases.

Problems over the use and life-times of fossil fuels have prompted a search for alternative ways of generating power. In the 1960s the first nuclear power stations were built. They seemed to be the answer to some of our problems. But some people think that the problem of disposing of the radioactive waste from these power stations is even greater than the problems caused by power stations that burn fossil fuels.

There are other ways of generating electricity, though – ways that do not consume limited resources. Figure 3 shows a hydroelectric power station in Sri Lanka. Hydroelectric power stations do not pose the same threat of pollution as fossil-fuel and nuclear power stations do. On the other hand, river valleys may have to be flooded to provide the water they need, and this has a big effect on the environment and its inhabitants.

Figure 4
Part of a biomass plant in Brazil, where fuel alcohol is extracted from fermented cane juice.

Figure 5
In the World Solar Challenge race in 1987, vehicles had to cross Australia using only energy from the Sun. The race was won by this car, *Sunraycer*, at an average speed of 66 kilometres per hour.

1 Suggest two situations in which a solar-powered electricity generator would be useful.

Figure 6
An oil rig in the hostile conditions of the North Sea.

The Sun has always been the main source of energy for this planet. The Sun's energy is continually being collected and stored in growing plants by a process called **photosynthesis** (see Unit F9). It is this process that has stored energy in coal, which is the fossilized remains of plants. In some sunny parts of the world, the Sun's energy is collected by raising quick-growing plants such as papyrus and sugar cane. The plants are then either used directly as fuel or are processed to make important chemicals. Such crops, together with wood chips and animal waste, can all be used as fuels. They are known collectively as **biomass** (see figure 4).

Scientists have now begun to solve the problem of using the Sun's energy directly to generate electricity (see figure 5). Energy resources such as the Sun, water, the tides and the wind are not 'used up' in the way fossil fuels are. For this reason, such resources are often called **renewable energy resources**.

Not all our energy needs can be satisfied by electricity. No one has yet managed to design an electric car that has the flexibility and power of the petrol- and diesel-fuelled vehicles of today. Since oil is so important for this purpose, it is important that we do not squander it in other ways.

2 Suggest some ways in which oil is used, other than for heating.

Whatever energy resource we choose, its use will always have some impact on the environment. This may be through polluting the air, generating toxic waste or using up large areas of land. The only real way to reduce this impact is to reduce the amount of energy we use.

3 The pictures in this unit illustrate six energy resources. Try to think of some more.

Topic **D Chemical patterns**

Here are three sets of photographs showing the effects that heating has on different substances. The notes underneath them will help you to see how to tell the difference between melting, burning and decomposing.

Melting

This is an example of **melting**. The moulding-metal melts when it is heated in the ladle.

The molten metal flows to take the shape of the mould. The metal cools in the mould and freezes solid. When the mould is split open, you see a casting made from the metal.

The only thing that has changed in the moulding-metal is its shape. Melting and freezing do not change the metal chemically. Energy is needed to heat up the metal and melt it, and then this energy is lost to the surroundings as the metal cools down and freezes.

Burning

This is an example of **burning**. Energy from the flame heats up the strip of magnesium ribbon until it starts to melt.

Then the magnesium catches fire and burns with a brilliant white light. The magnesium reacts with oxygen in the air and turns into something new.

The white ash is called magnesium oxide. Burning is an example of a **chemical reaction**. Notice that the reaction gives out a great deal of energy.

42

Decomposing

(*Safety note*: mercury vapour is very poisonous, so this experiment must be done in a fume-cupboard that is known to be efficient.)

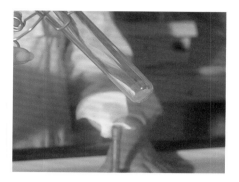

This is an example of heating being used to split up a chemical. Another word for 'splitting up' is **decomposing.** The orange powder in the test-tube is mercury oxide.

Heating changes the solid powder – the first signs are shiny grey droplets on the side of the test-tube. They are drops of mercury, which is a liquid.

The glowing-splint test tells you that something else is happening too. The glowing splint bursts into flame, showing that oxygen gas has been formed. Heating has split up mercury oxide into mercury and oxygen.

Here is another set of photographs, showing the effects of heating sugar. Look at the pictures carefully and see if you can decide what is happening. Remember that there might be more than one change (magnesium, for example, starts to melt before it burns).

Describe the changes that happen as sugar is heated. Is the sugar melting, burning or decomposing?

What is the chemical recipe for a human body? One answer to this question is given on this page. Figure 1 shows what you would get if you could break down a person into the simple chemicals that we call **elements**.

1.5 kg of nitrogen, N : the volume of this quantity of nitrogen gas would normally be about 1.3 m³

32.5 kg of oxygen, O : the volume of this quantity of oxygen gas would normally be about 24 m³ (enough to fill a small room)

5 kg of hydrogen, H : the volume of this quantity of hydrogen gas would normally be about 60 m³

9 kg of carbon, C

1 kg of calcium, Ca

500 g of phosphorus, P

175 g of potassium, K

125 g of sulphur, S

75 g of sodium, Na

25 g of magnesium, Mg

75 g of chlorine, Cl : the volume of this quantity of chlorine gas would normally be about 0.025 m³ (25 litres)

2 g of iron, Fe

Figure 1
This is what you would get if you could break down a 50 kg girl into her chemical elements. There would be small traces of other elements as well, including iodine, fluorine and silicon — you would find more than 30 elements in all. The strange thing is that some of these elements are gases — how can a solid person be made up of gases? You will be able to understand this better when you have found out more about the chemistry of water.

Why are the elements 'simple'?

Unit A3 describes the theory which says that everything is made up of very small particles.

- Everything is made up of very small particles.
- Everything is made up of elements.

What is the link between the small particles and the chemical elements? The link lies in the word 'atom'. The first person to say this in a modern way was John Dalton (see figure 2).

In Dalton's theory, the very small particles of an element are **atoms**. Each element has its own kind of atom. Copper is made up of only copper atoms (see figure 3), and iron is made up of only iron atoms. The elements are chemically simple because they each contain only their own atoms.

In some elements, the atoms are joined together in small groups. Oxygen atoms, for instance, usually go around in pairs. Small groups of atoms are called **molecules** (see Unit D4).

Safe as part of the body but dangerous when free

The elements in figure 1 are quite safe when they are part of a human body but some of them can be very dangerous when they are free. For example, the element phosphorus on its own can be very harmful (especially in a form called 'white phosphorus', which gives off poisonous fumes) and yet we are quite safe with 500 g of phosphorus in our bodies.

White phosphorus was once used to make matches. In the 1880s, there were 700 girls making matches in a factory in London, some of them only six years old. Many of the girls developed a horrible disease called 'phossy jaw' because the phosphorus fumes made their jaw-bones rot.

In 1888 Annie Besant published a fierce article about the working conditions of the matchgirls. She did not think that they had the power to defend themselves but, to her surprise, the girls went on strike. She was then able to raise money to help them, and eventually the factory owners agreed to listen to their complaints. This was the first industrial victory gained by unskilled workers seeking better working conditions. The use of white phosphorus in matches was banned by law in 1908. Since then, more controls have been introduced to protect people from other harmful raw materials and chemicals.

Look at the elements in figure 1. List them in two columns, as metals and non-metals. How do you recognize the metals? Are any of them hard to classify?

Figure 2
Dalton was led to his atomic theory by his study of gases. Here he is shown collecting marsh gas (methane) by stirring the bottom of a pond.

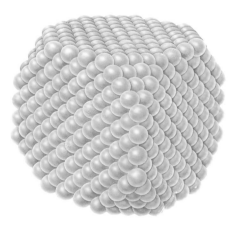

Figure 3
Atoms in a crystal of the element copper. All the atoms are the same – they are all copper atoms.

Figure 4
Members of the Matchmakers' Union who were successful in their strike against appalling conditions and low wages in 1888.

45

D3 Mixing and joining

Figure 1

a Here the cook is measuring out the ingredients for a cake and then mixing them.

b Now she is pouring the mixture of butter, sugar, flour, milk and eggs into a baking tin.

c Now you cannot see flour, butter and eggs. Heating has combined them into something new.

How can so many things in the world about us all be made from only about a hundred elements? Comparing chemistry with cooking may help with the answer. A cook can use a few ingredients to prepare many different dishes. For example, she can use fat, sugar, eggs, flour and milk to make a cake (see figure 1). We can write

$$\text{fat} + \text{sugar} + \text{eggs} + \text{flour} + \text{milk} \xrightarrow{\text{join together when baked}} \text{cake}$$

The cook could also have used the same ingredients to make other things, such as biscuits, scones, batter or pastry.

Figure 2 shows you an example of *chemical* cookery. The ingredients are two elements which are first mixed and then joined by heating. The chemist is mixing grey zinc with yellow sulphur. Using fine powders makes it easier to mix them up well.

Figure 2
The chemical reaction between zinc and sulphur, which you may be shown. The reaction can sometimes be unexpectedly violent.

Zinc – a metal element

Sulphur – a non-metal element

Mixing zinc and sulphur – if you look closely, you can still see separate grains of the two elements

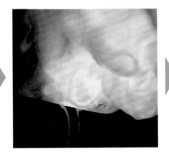

Zinc and sulphur combine violently on heating

The compound, zinc sulphide is something new – you cannot see zinc or sulphur any more

A word equation is a shorthand way of writing down what happens during a chemical reaction:

$$\text{zinc} + \text{sulphur} \longrightarrow \text{zinc sulphide}$$

46

Table salt is a familiar compound. We use it in cooking and we sprinkle it on our food. Table salt is a **compound** of two elements – it is made from sodium and chlorine. The chemical name for salt is sodium chloride. Figure 3 shows sodium and chlorine reacting to make salt. We can write the reaction as a word equation:

sodium + chlorine $\longrightarrow$ sodium chloride

The names of *two-element* compounds end in 'ide'.

Figure 3
a Sodium metal and chlorine gas.   **b** Sodium reacting with chlorine.   **c** Sodium chloride.

Millions of compounds from about a hundred elements

Another way of thinking about elements and compounds is to compare them with the letters of the alphabet and the words in this book. There are only 26 letters but they can be joined in different ways to make thousands of words.

The words only make sense if the right letters are joined in the right order. There are two-letter words such as 'in', 'on' and 'to', and three-letter words such as 'the', 'car' and 'box'. But there are also words with many letters, such as 'pressure', 'photosynthesis' and 'crystal'.

Chemical compounds, like words, are made by joining elements in the right way. There are compounds with two, three and many elements joined together. Some are solids; others are liquids or gases.

Figure 4
Nitrogen dioxide is a brown gas. It is a two-element compound.

Figure 5
Sugar: a three-element compound. The three elements are carbon, hydrogen and oxygen.

Figure 6
Hexane is one of the liquids in petrol. Hexane is a two-element compound in which carbon and hydrogen are joined together.

Figure 7
Garnet: a many-element compound. It is a compound of aluminium, silicon, oxygen, calcium, magnesium and iron.

47

D4 What happens when hydrogen burns?

Looking at figure 1 on page 44, you may have wondered how the human body can be made up of so much oxygen and hydrogen – how is it possible? The answer is that the two gases are not present as free elements in our bodies, but are joined as chemical compounds. When elements combine, they change into something quite new.

A mixture of hydrogen and oxygen can explode if you light it. It does not have to do this, though. In the apparatus in figure 1 the change is happening in a controlled way. Plenty of energy is still released, but now the result is a very hot flame.

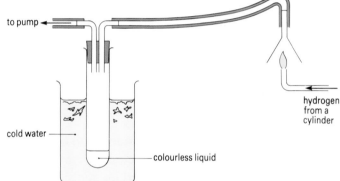

Figure 1

These two pictures both show hydrogen reacting with oxygen. The hydrogen comes from a cylinder. The hydrogen burns at the end of the glass tube by reacting with oxygen in the air. The products of the reaction are drawn into the glass funnel by a pump. The hot gases cool in the test-tube surrounded by cold water. Gradually, a colourless liquid collects at the bottom of the cold tube.

Testing the liquid made by burning hydrogen in oxygen

Figures 2 and 3 show the results of some tests on the liquid that is made, and on some other colourless liquids. What do they tell you about the reaction of hydrogen with oxygen?

Figure 2

a A drop of the liquid collected in the apparatus in figure 1 has been put onto some blue cobalt chloride paper.

b Here is another piece of cobalt chloride paper which has had a drop of water put on it.

c A drop of hexane (see figure 6 on page 47) was put onto this piece of cobalt chloride paper.

48

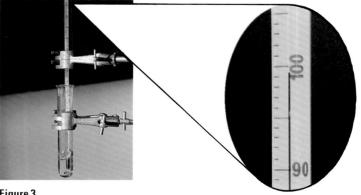

Figure 3
The liquid in this tube was made by burning hydrogen in oxygen. The liquid is boiling. You can read off the boiling-point from the thermometer. Now look at the table of boiling-points in figure 4.

Colourless liquid	Boiling-point (°C)
Ethanol	78
Hexane	69
Propanone	56
Water	100

Figure 4
Boiling-points of some colourless liquids.

New molecules for old!

The theory of atoms and molecules can give us a picture of what happens when hydrogen reacts with oxygen (see figure 5).

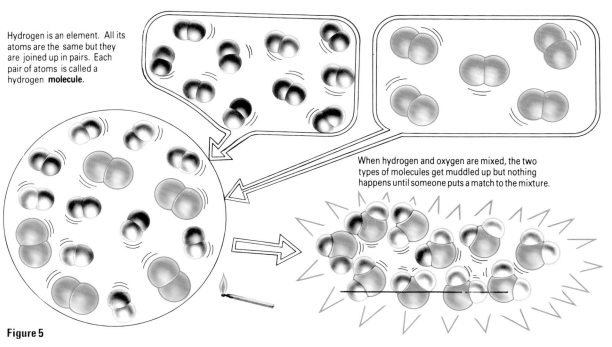

Hydrogen is an element. All its atoms are the same but they are joined up in pairs. Each pair of atoms is called a hydrogen **molecule**.

Oxygen is an element, so its atoms are all the same too. These atoms are joined up in pairs to form oxygen molecules

When hydrogen and oxygen are mixed, the two types of molecules get muddled up but nothing happens until someone puts a match to the mixture.

In the heat of the flame the two gases react. The hydrogen molecules and the oxygen molecules split up and join together in a new way to make water molecules.

Figure 5

Water is a two-element compound. We could call it *hydrogen oxide*, but we usually use the everyday name.

hydrogen + oxygen $\longrightarrow$ water (hydrogen oxide)

Notice that water is quite different from hydrogen or oxygen. Analysis of a human body shows up plenty of hydrogen and oxygen because it contains so much water.

Ice, water and steam are different states of the same compound. The molecules are the same in all three states, but they are arranged in different ways. You now know that the particles in figure 3 on page 7 are really water molecules.

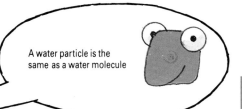

A water particle is the same as a water molecule

49

D5 Thousands of hydrocarbons

You may have been surprised to learn that all the materials in the world about us are made from only about a hundred elements. What is even more strange is that there are thousands of compounds which are made by joining just the *two* elements hydrogen and carbon. Figures 1 to 3 will give you an idea of the range.

Figure 1
Natural gas is the simplest hydrocarbon. Its chemical name is **methane**.

Figure 2
Petrol is a mixture of many different hydrocarbons. One of them is **hexane**.

Figure 3
Candle wax is also a mixture of hydrocarbons. One of the hydrocarbons in the wax is **eicosane**.

We call all these compounds **hydrocarbons**. We can only explain why there are so many different hydrocarbons by thinking about atoms and molecules (see figure 4).

Methane is the simplest hydrocarbon, with one carbon atom in its molecules. There are four hydrogen atoms linked to the carbon atom and the chemical formula for this molecule is written CH_4.

In a hexane molecule there are six carbon atoms in a chain, with fourteen hydrogen atoms joined to them. The numbers of carbon and hydrogen atoms are shown in the formula for hexane, which is C_6H_{14}.

The hydrocarbons with one, two, three or four carbon atoms in their molecules are normally gases. The compounds with bigger molecules, such as hexane, are liquids. Compounds with even bigger molecules are solids, such as eicosane which has twenty carbon atoms in each molecule.

Figure 4
Models of methane, hexane and eicosane molecules. In these models, the carbon atoms are shown as black spheres and the hydrogen atoms as white ones.

a methane molecule, CH_4

a hexane molecule, C_6H_{14}

an eicosane molecule, $C_{20}H_{42}$

Sorting out molecules according to size

We get most of our hydrocarbons from crude oil. Crude oil is a dark oily liquid which is made up of many different hydrocarbons. Before we can use it, we have to separate it into useful parts, called **fractions**.

Oil refining is a complicated process. Refineries carry out a series of steps to separate and purify the many products. The key step is **fractional distillation**. Oil is heated in a furnace and piped into a tall tower called a **fractionating column** (see figure 7). The column is hotter at the bottom and cooler near the top. Gases, such as methane, travel up the column and are collected at the top. Hydrocarbons with bigger molecules, such as hexane, rise until the column is cool enough for them to condense to liquids. The liquids collected from the column at various heights are the fractions. Each fraction contains molecules that are about the same size.

Fractional distillation sorts out the molecules in oil according to their size. The smaller the molecules, the lower the boiling-point and the higher they rise in the column before they condense. The process is the first step on the way to making fuels such as petrol and paraffin. It also sorts out the hydrocarbons needed to manufacture plastics, dyes, farm chemicals, medicines, detergents and cosmetics.

Figure 5
Crude oil.

Figure 6
Aviation fuel.

Figure 7
Fractional distillation is the first of a series of processes for making fuels and chemicals.

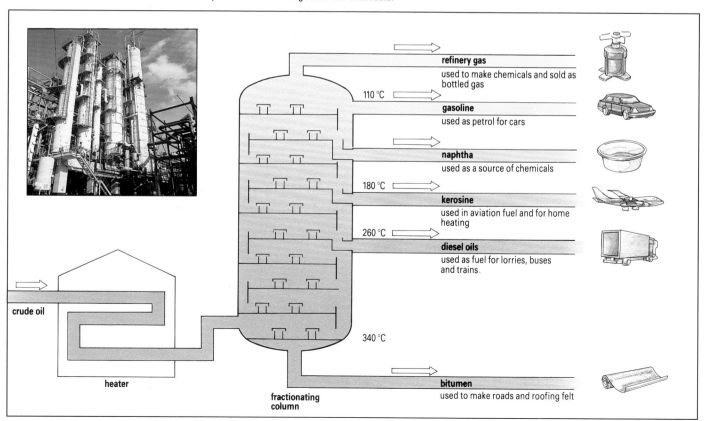

refinery gas
used to make chemicals and sold as bottled gas

110 °C

gasoline
used as petrol for cars

naphtha
used as a source of chemicals

180 °C

kerosine
used in aviation fuel and for home heating

260 °C

diesel oils
used as fuel for lorries, buses and trains.

crude oil

340 °C

heater

fractionating column

bitumen
used to make roads and roofing felt

How useful it would be if we could have a map to guide us round the chemistry of the elements – something that could quickly show us where to find the metals or the non-metals, a map that could tell us where to find elements that are reactive, or precious, or poisonous.

Such a map does exist. We call it the Periodic Table and you will probably have seen copies of it on the walls of science laboratories.

The elements in the Periodic Table are placed in order of their atomic masses. Hydrogen atoms are the lightest atoms so they come first, followed by helium, lithium, beryllium and so on. Figure 4 shows part of the Periodic Table up to element number 54, which is xenon. So the element with the heaviest atoms in figure 4 is xenon.

Figure 1
Dmitri Mendeleev discovered the Periodic Table. He worked out how to arrange the elements before they had all been discovered. He left gaps in his table and predicted the properties of the missing elements. Chemists were very impressed when these missing elements were discovered and they were found to fit the gaps.

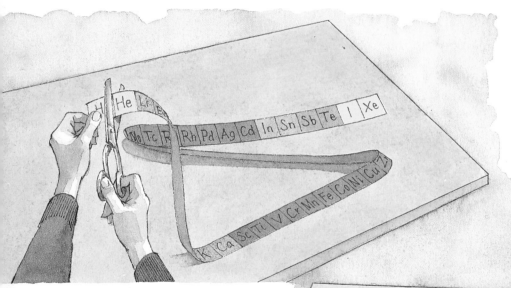

Figure 2
Here is a long strip of paper with the element symbols on it starting with hydrogen. You can imagine this strip being cut up and glued into place to make the Periodic Table.

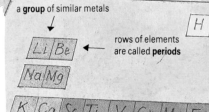

Figure 3
Here the Periodic Table is being built up by gluing down the cut-up strips of elements from figure 2. The strips are arranged so that similar elements are close together.

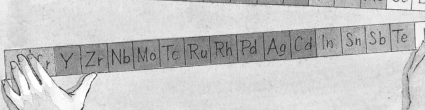

group 1   2

| | | | | | | | | | | | | | | 3 | 4 | 5 | 6 | 7 | 8 |

group 1	2													3	4	5	6	7	8
							1 H												2 He
3 Li	4 Be													5 B	6 C	7 N	8 O	9 F	10 Ne
11 Na	12 Mg													13 Al	14 Si	15 P	16 S	17 Cl	18 Ar
19 K	20 Ca	21 Sc	22 Ti	23 V	24 Cr	25 Mn	26 Fe	27 Co	28 Ni	29 Cu	30 Zn			31 Ga	32 Ge	33 As	34 Se	35 Br	36 Kr
37 Rb	38 Sr	39 Y	40 Zr	41 Nb	42 Mo	43 Tc	44 Ru	45 Rh	46 Pd	47 Ag	48 Cd			49 In	50 Sn	51 Sb	52 Te	53 I	54 Xe

Figure 4
The Periodic Table, showing the first 54 elements. The elements are numbered starting with the element with the lightest atoms, which is hydrogen. These numbers are shown in red and are called the **atomic numbers** of the elements. All the non-metals are on the right of the table. They are coloured yellow. You can find out more about the group 7 elements on page 55.

Figure 5
All the metals come together on the left of the Periodic Table. In figure 4 they are coloured blue. You can find out more about the group 1 metals on page 54.

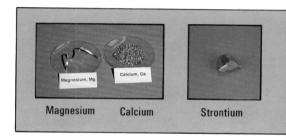
Magnesium   Calcium   Strontium

Figure 6
Germanium, arsenic, antimony and tellurium are hard to classify. In some ways they are like metals but in other ways they are like non-metals. These 'in-between' elements are coloured green in figure 4.

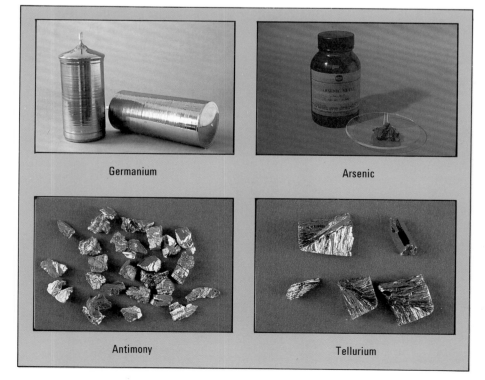
Germanium   Arsenic

Antimony   Tellurium

Figure 7
The metals in the block shaded the darker blue in figure 4 are called the **transition metals**. This block includes precious metals such as copper, silver and gold.

53

D7 Families of elements

Figure 1

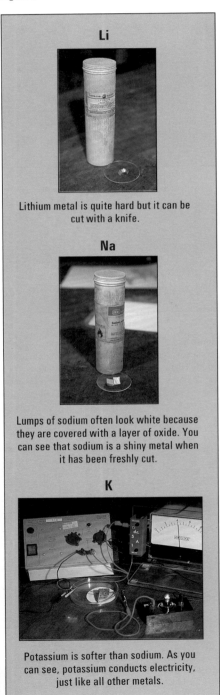

Li

Lithium metal is quite hard but it can be cut with a knife.

Na

Lumps of sodium often look white because they are covered with a layer of oxide. You can see that sodium is a shiny metal when it has been freshly cut.

K

Potassium is softer than sodium. As you can see, potassium conducts electricity, just like all other metals.

The alkali metals

Elements in the same group in the Periodic Table have similar properties. If you look at the left-hand side of the Periodic Table on page 53, you will see a column of metals which are all highly reactive. They have to be kept in oil to stop them reacting with the air. The family name of this group is the **alkali metals** because they form many alkaline compounds.

Unlike most other metals, the alkali metals float on water. They react with water too. This word equation describes the violent reaction of potassium with water (see figure 2):

$$\text{potassium(s)} + \text{water(l)} \longrightarrow \text{potassium hydroxide(aq)} + \text{hydrogen(g)}$$

Figure 2
Small pieces of potassium react so violently with water that the hydrogen formed catches fire. The flame is coloured mauve by the potassium. The solution formed is very alkaline.

Figure 3
This picture shows street lighting in Helsinki, Finland. The yellow lamps contain sodium.

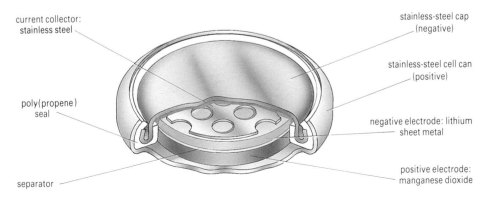

current collector: stainless steel

stainless-steel cap (negative)

stainless-steel cell can (positive)

poly(propene) seal

negative electrode: lithium sheet metal

separator

positive electrode: manganese dioxide

Figure 4
This small electric battery is made using lithium. This type of battery is used in watches and calculators.

The halogens

Elements in the same group are similar but not identical. This is clearly shown by the three elements in group 7, which are shown in figure 5. You can see that the elements are similar because they all give coloured vapours but that the colours are different.

Another way in which the elements are similar is the way in which they all react with metals. Figure 3 on page 47 shows chlorine reacting with sodium to make sodium chloride. Bromine and iodine react in a similar way. Figure 6 on this page shows that sodium bromide and sodium iodide look very similar to sodium chloride.

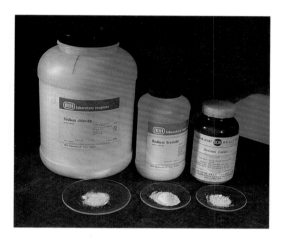

Figure 6
The salt we put on our food is a compound of sodium and chlorine called sodium chloride. Bromine and iodine form similar compounds with sodium, and these are called 'salts' too. The name 'halogen' means 'salt-former' The halogens form salts with many metals.

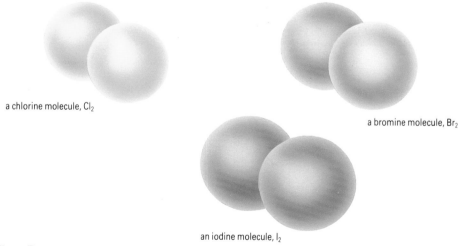

a chlorine molecule, Cl_2

a bromine molecule, Br_2

an iodine molecule, I_2

Figure 7
Models of halogen molecules.

Chlorine, bromine and iodine are all very reactive, so much so that they can kill living things. Chlorine, for example, is used to kill bacteria in drinking water.

The atoms in chlorine, bromine and iodine are arranged in similar ways: in all three elements they are joined in pairs (see figure 7).

Figure 5

Cl

Chlorine is a greenish-yellow gas at room temperature.

Br

Bromine is a dark red liquid. The liquid evaporates easily, giving an orange-brown vapour.

I

Iodine is a grey solid but on gentle warming it gives off a deep purple vapour.

D8 Alkalis and acids

Alkalis

Alkalis are just as important as acids are. We use alkalis to wash up after meals and there is alkali in the toothpaste we use to clean our teeth. Farmers spread alkali on their fields to make sure that the soil is in a good condition to grow crops. Industry uses alkalis to manufacture bleach, soap and glass. Alkalis are used to purify water and to make it fit to drink.

Most common alkalis are compounds of reactive metals (see figure 2). The easiest way to spot an alkali is to dissolve it in water and test the solution with an indicator.

Alkaline solutions turn litmus paper blue. On the pH scale, they have numbers above 7. The strongest alkalis are compounds of the alkali metals, such as sodium hydroxide.

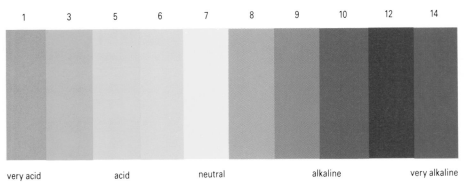

Figure 1
The colours of an indicator paper used to measure the pH of acid and alkaline solutions.

group 1	group 2
LiOH lithium hydroxide	
NaOH sodium hydroxide	**Mg(OH)₂** magnesium hydroxide
KOH potassium hydroxide	**Ca(OH)₂** calcium hydroxide

Figure 2

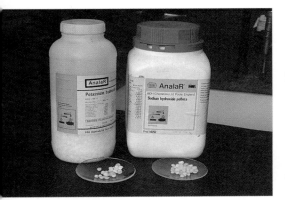

Figure 3
Pellets of sodium hydroxide and potassium hydroxide. Both these alkalis are highly **caustic**. Anything caustic is highly corrosive and will eat into your flesh.

Figure 4
Alkalis are used to turn fats into soap. A mixture of fats is heated in a large vat with an alkali such as sodium hydroxide.

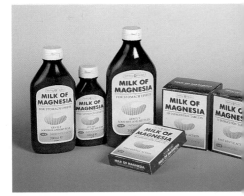

Figure 5
Magnesium hydroxide is used to make antacid tablets. 'Ant-acid' means 'against acid'. Antacid tablets **neutralize** acid in your stomach (see page 58).

Acids

The word 'acid' sounds dangerous! The common laboratory acids, such as hydrochloric acid and sulphuric acid, are dangerous when they are concentrated. Handle them with care even when dilute.

You can easily test a solution to see if it is acid by using an indicator paper. Litmus paper turns red in acid solutions. Acid solutions have pH numbers below 7 – the more acid the solution, the *lower* the pH.

Notice that acids are compounds of non-metals, on the right of the Periodic Table (see figure 7). Many of them are formed when non-metal oxides, for example carbon dioxide, dissolve in water:

carbon dioxide(g) + water(l) ⟶ carbonic acid (aq)

Carbonated water and fizzy drinks taste sharp because they contain carbonic acid.

Figure 6
Hydrofluoric acid is a very dangerous compound. It is one of the few chemicals which can attack glass. This glass was etched with the acid.

group 3	group 4	group 5	group 6	group 7	group 8
	H_2CO_3 carbonic acid	HNO_3 nitric acid		HF hydrofluoric acid	
		H_3PO_4 phosphoric acid	H_2SO_4 sulphuric acid	HCl hydrochloric acid	

Figure 7

Figure 8
Here are some acids you might find at home. Citric acid gives oranges and lemons their sharp taste. Acetic acid (which chemists call ethanoic acid) is the main ingredient of vinegar.

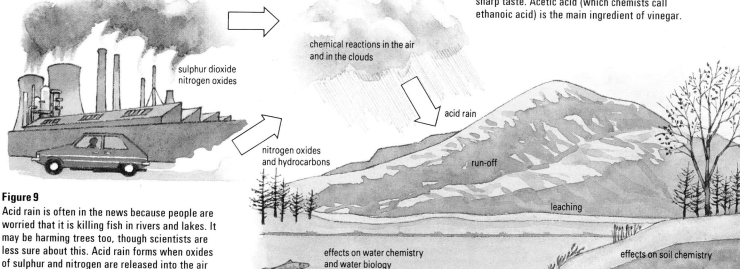

Figure 9
Acid rain is often in the news because people are worried that it is killing fish in rivers and lakes. It may be harming trees too, though scientists are less sure about this. Acid rain forms when oxides of sulphur and nitrogen are released into the air from engines, factories and power stations. The oxides react with water and oxygen to form sulphuric acid and nitric acid.

57

D9 Salts

Figure 1
Most plants grow best if the soil is very slightly acid (about pH 6.5). This Brazilian farmer is spreading lime to stop the soil getting too acid.

The farmer in figure 1 is worried that his soil is getting too acid, so he is spreading lime on his fields. The lime is an alkali which reacts with the acid and **neutralizes** it. In a similar way, toothpaste contains an alkali which neutralizes acids in our mouths to stop them destroying our teeth.

There are many examples of this chemical change that we call neutralization. But what happens to the acid when it is neutralized? The answer is that it turns into a **salt**. In chemistry, the word 'salt' does not mean just the sodium chloride we sprinkle on our food. It also covers very many other compounds which can be made from acids and alkalis.

Neutralization

There is a pattern to neutralization reactions, which is shown by this word equation:

$$alkali + acid \longrightarrow salt + water$$

You can see more easily how the alkali neutralizes the acid with an example written in words and chemical symbols. Look carefully and you will notice that the atoms in the acid and alkali have been rearranged to make two new compounds which are neutral: sodium chloride and water.

$$sodium\ hydroxide + hydrochloric\ acid \longrightarrow sodium\ chloride + water$$
$$NaOH + HCl \longrightarrow NaCl + H_2O$$

You can think of salts as having two parents: a parent alkali and a parent acid. This idea is illustrated in figures 2 and 3.

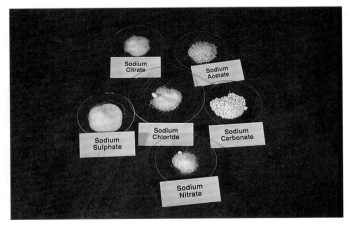

Figure 2
All these salts can be made by neutralizing the alkali sodium hydroxide with different acids. They are all **sodium salts**.

Figure 3
All these salts can be made by neutralizing sulphuric acid. They are all **sulphates**.

Salt crystals

Salts can be found naturally as minerals. Sometimes they are discovered in the form of beautiful crystals, as shown in figures 4, 5 and 6. You may have tried to grow large salt crystals from solution or watched crystals growing under a microscope. Figures 7 and 8 show some fine examples of crystals grown from solution and of what you can see.

Figure 4
Fluorite is mined in the Peak District, where it is sometimes found in a form called Blue John. The chemical name of fluorite is calcium fluoride.

Figure 5
Barytes feels surprisingly heavy when you lift it, so it is sometimes called 'heavy spar'. Chemically, it consists of barium sulphate.

Figure 6
This alabaster effigy of Edward II is made from one form of the mineral called gypsum. Gypsum consists of the salt called calcium sulphate.

Figure 7
Salt crystals grown from solution.

a Alum.

b Copper sulphate.

Figure 8
Crystals seen growing on microscope slides.

a Potassium nitrate.

b Ammonium chloride.

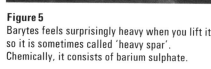

1 Try to find out the chemical names of the salts in the following: Epsom salts, washing soda, plaster of Paris, calamine lotion, Bordeaux mixture, baking powder, chalk.

2 What can you discover about the uses of these salts: barium sulphate, copper sulphate, iron sulphate, sodium hydrogensulphate, potassium chlorate, ammonium nitrate, potassium nitrate, silver bromide?

PROPERTY WORDS

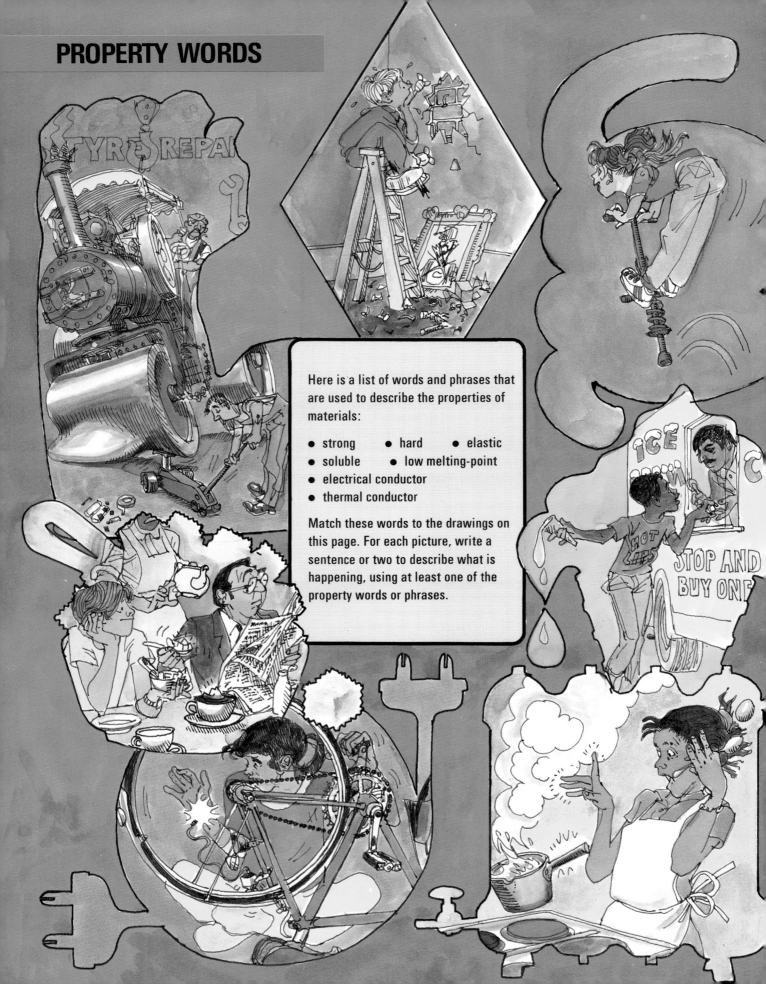

Here is a list of words and phrases that are used to describe the properties of materials:

- strong
- hard
- elastic
- soluble
- low melting-point
- electrical conductor
- thermal conductor

Match these words to the drawings on this page. For each picture, write a sentence or two to describe what is happening, using at least one of the property words or phrases.

Topic **E** **Weather and landscape**

Figure 1
'What will it do today?'

Figure 2
A meteorologist taking temperature readings.
Why do you think the boxes have slots all round
them?

'Do you think it will rain before we get back? Shall we take an umbrella?'
'Is it too windy to fly my kite?'
'Shall we pack the sun-tan lotion?'

How many times have you asked questions like these? They are all
questions about the weather. People who live in the British Isles are well
known for their conversations about the weather – it is often something of
a joke in other countries. In Britain, the weather is very changeable and
may seem unpredictable, but it is not like that everywhere in the world. In
this topic you will find out more about the weather and about the work of
meteorologists (scientists who study weather patterns).

Wind is an important feature of our weather. Someone once said that
wind was 'air in a hurry'. Why should air be in a hurry? Is something
pushing it? Perhaps we will be able to answer these questions once we
have found out a bit more about air itself.

We live at the bottom of a 'sea' of air which is about 1600 km deep (see
figure 3). This 'sea' of air is called the **atmosphere**. It is only in the lowest
11 km that the 'weather' occurs.

At ground level there is 1600 km of air pressing down on us. The
atmosphere presses on every square metre of ground with a force of
approximately 100 000 newtons (that is the same weight as a large car).
This force on each square metre is called the **atmospheric pressure** at
ground level. It is about 100 000 newtons per square metre (N/m²).
Meteorologists prefer to use a special pressure unit, called the **millibar**
(mb). 1000 millibars is the same as 100 000 newtons per square metre. But
the atmospheric pressure is not constant and unchanging: it varies from
place to place and from time to time. And it doesn't just act downwards,
but in all directions.

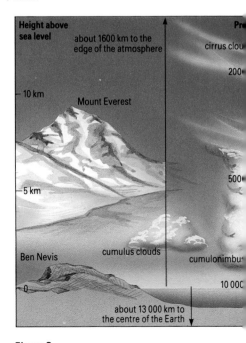

Height above sea level — about 1600 km to the edge of the atmosphere — cirrus clou — 200 — 10 km — Mount Everest — 5 km — 500 — Ben Nevis — cumulus clouds — cumulonimbu — 0 — 10 00 — about 13 000 km to the centre of the Earth

Figure 3
A diagram of the atmosphere. Look how 'deep' it
is compared with some mountains.

'Highs' and 'lows'

Atmospheric pressure is measured using a barometer (see figure 4). You may already have seen one at school, or you may have one at home.

At fixed times every day, readings are taken from barometers at many places over the surface of the Earth. The meteorologists plot these readings on a map and then draw smooth lines on the map to join together places with the same pressure. This gives a **pressure map** like the one in figure 5. The lines are called **isobars**. The isobars form closed loops around centres of high or low pressure. They look very much like the contour lines on an ordinary map (see figure 6).

Areas of high pressure are called 'highs' or 'anticyclones', and areas of low pressure are known as 'lows' or 'depressions'. A high- or low-pressure area may extend over many thousands of square kilometres. Figure 5 shows a 'high' covering the British Isles with a 'low' to the west of Ireland.

> How large is the difference in pressure between the centres of the 'high' and the 'low' in figure 5?

Differences in pressure force air to move from areas where the pressure is high towards other areas where the pressure is low. As the air moves from a 'high' to a 'low', it has to move across the surface of the Earth, which is itself spinning quickly on a north–south axis. The result is that the air doesn't flow straight from the 'high' to the 'low', at right angles to the isobars on the pressure map, but at an angle to them. In the Northern Hemisphere, the winds blow so that the air spirals in a clockwise direction *out of* a 'high' and in an anticlockwise direction *into* a 'low' (see figure 7).

Figure 4
Household barometer.

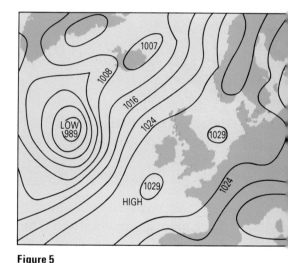

Figure 5
A pressure map of the British Isles.

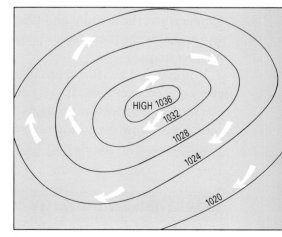

Figure 7
Air spiralling clockwise out of an anticyclone in the Northern Hemisphere. (The pressures are given in millibars.)

Figure 6
The contour lines on a map link places at the same height in the same way as isobars link places with the same pressure.

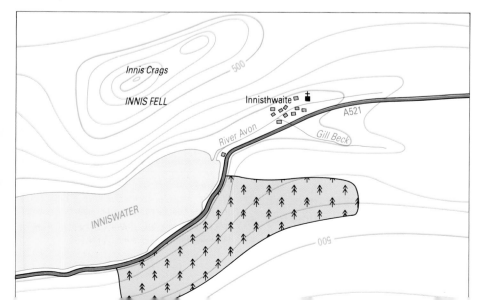

63

E2 The weather and energy

Pressure maps can give us information about the speed and direction of winds. Where there is a large pressure difference between two places that are fairly close together, we expect high winds or even gales. Such winds can do a great deal of damage (see figure 1).

Meteorologists have found that these pressure maps can give them much more information about the weather than just the speeds and directions of the winds. Some types of pressure patterns are more likely to give rain than others, and other types are often associated with fine sunny weather. Pressure maps can be made even more useful if other details are added to them, for instance the wind direction and speed, the air temperature, the amount and type of cloud, the visibility (how far you can see) and how the pressure is changing. Such maps are then referred to as **weather maps**.

You can find weather maps in most newspapers and you can see them every day on television. If you compare one day's map with the next, you can see how the pressure systems have moved in the last 24 hours. You can also see how the weather has changed. Figure 2 shows two newspaper weather maps for midday on 20th and 21st July 1988.

Weather and energy

One-half of the Earth's surface is facing towards the Sun at all times. The day-time half is receiving energy radiated by the Sun; the night-time half is not.

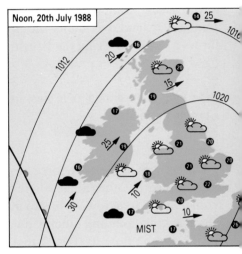

Figure 1
The damage weather can do.

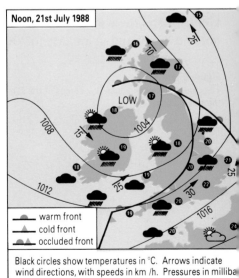

Black circles show temperatures in °C. Arrows indicate wind directions, with speeds in km/h. Pressures in milliba

Figure 2
Weather maps for successive days in 1988. Make a table to compare the weather near where you live on 21st July with that on 20th July. Put as much detail into your table as you can.

Not all the energy that falls on the day-time half of the Earth reaches the ground. Some wavelengths of the radiation are absorbed by gases in the atmosphere. A layer of ozone at a height of around 20 to 25 km absorbs nearly all the harmful ultra-violet radiation, for example. Most of the visible and infra-red radiation gets through the atmosphere without warming it up as it passes through. When this radiation reaches the clouds and the ground, some is reflected back into space. The rest (about 70 per cent) is absorbed at the surface. Some of this causes water to evaporate, so there is always some water vapour mixed with the air. Some of the energy is used in photosynthesis. But most simply warms up the ground. It is this energy which is transferred to the air around us.

How does this transfer happen? Try sitting on a warm surface – a hot beach, say – and you will soon feel the result as some of the energy stored in the shingle is transferred to your cooler body. That is an example of the **conduction** of energy from something warm to something cooler.

Figure 3
Only one-half of the Earth receives energy from the Sun at any one time.

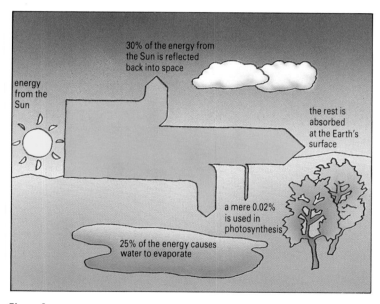

Figure 4
What happens to the Sun's energy when it falls on the Earth.

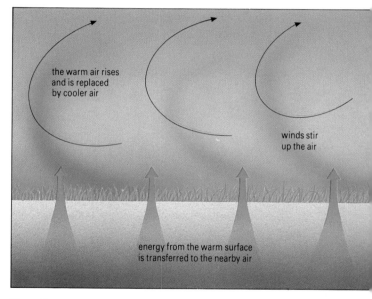

Figure 5
How energy is transferred from the Earth's surface to the air.

This is the way in which energy is transferred from the warmed surface of the Earth to the layer of air right 'next door'. This layer of air warms up and its temperature rises. The wind, and upward currents, will quickly move this warmer air away from the surface and replace it with another lot of cooler air. This, in its turn, warms up. So energy is transferred from the warm surface into the surrounding air. As the air is stirred up by the wind, the warmed air mixes with the cooler air. The energy is spread out through very large masses of air.

Water vapour evaporated from the seas and lakes, or transpired by plants, gets mixed up with the air of the atmosphere in the same way. In warm, damp or humid climates, as much as 4 per cent of the atmosphere is water vapour; in cold climates or over deserts there is far, far less.

Find three areas of the world where the climate is **a** warm and humid, **b** cold and dry, and **c** hot and dry. What sort of weather do these three places have? How is the weather related to the amount of water vapour in the atmosphere?

E3 Convection and the weather

One of the things the energy from the Sun does is to evaporate water. But the atmosphere can't go on taking up more and more water. It is a bit like a sponge – eventually it becomes saturated, so that it will hold no more water vapour.

The quantity of water vapour the air will hold depends on its temperature. Cold air won't hold much, but warm air will hold a great deal more. What matters to meteorologists is not so much *how much* water there is in the atmosphere, but how close it is to saturation. The term meteorologists use to describe this is **relative humidity**. Air which can hold no more water vapour is said to have 100 per cent relative humidity. Air with 50 per cent relative humidity is only holding half the amount of water vapour that it might do.

If saturated air cools down, it will be unable to hold all its water vapour, and some will condense into droplets of water. If this happens at ground level, we have a **mist** or **fog** (see figure 1). If it occurs above ground level, we have **clouds**.

Figure 1
Mist is formed when saturated air cools down.

1 Kitchen and bathroom windows often 'mist up' in use. What is it that is condensing on the misted windows? What can you say about the humidity of the air in the room? What can you say about the temperature of the window glass?

2 The cumulus clouds in figure 2 have bases which are quite flat and are all at the same level. What can you say about the temperature and the humidity at that level?

Figure 2
Cumulus clouds.

How clouds are formed

Look at the photograph (figure 2) of the 'fluffy heap' clouds, which are called **cumulus** clouds. They are also known as **convection** clouds, because convection is a very important process in their formation.

A hot-air balloon is a good example of the use of convection in the atmosphere. For a balloon to float, the average density of the balloon, the air inside it, the basket and so on must be equal to the density of the air around it.

For the balloon to rise, the balloonist must reduce the density of the air inside it. He does this by burning some of the gas and so warming the air. Convection then lifts the balloon to a higher level.

Figure 3
The gas burner is used to warm up the air inside the balloon.

3 After the burner has been switched off, the balloon will stop rising. What can you say about the average densities of the balloon and the air surrounding it then? When the balloon stops rising, how big is the force pushing it upwards?

In just the same way, convection can take place in the atmosphere itself. The air over any warm surface will warm up. It becomes less dense than the surrounding air and so is pushed up by the colder, denser air. It will rise, just like the balloon. Cooler air from above flows in to take the place of the rising warm air. Convection has started.

As the warm air rises through the atmosphere, the pressure around it falls. This allows the warm air to expand, which in turn causes it to cool down. When the air has cooled enough for its relative humidity to reach 100 per cent, cloud droplets are very likely to form.

Sometimes conditions in the atmosphere will allow a convection current of air to go up and up – perhaps to a height of several hundred kilometres. When this happens, the vertical speed of the air current may reach as much as 70 kilometres per hour. The huge cumulus clouds that are formed may give heavy rain or hail showers and even lightning.

Cumulus clouds are a visible sign of upward air currents. Both glider pilots and soaring birds of prey are aware of this and use such currents. If the up-current is a very strong one, a glider pilot may be in danger. Glider pilots are trained to recognize and avoid such extreme conditions.

In the clear air between cumulus clouds, cooler air will flow downwards, sometimes very quickly. These up- and down-currents really stir up the air. They take smoke and other pollutants, as well as water vapour, high in the atmosphere. Some of these pollutants may go even higher, entering the upper atmosphere and damaging the ozone layer.

Figure 4
Using convection.

a Bird of prey.

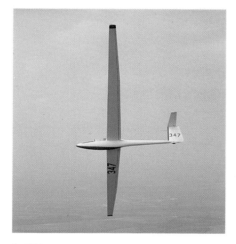

b Glider.

Figure 5
How cumulus clouds grow.

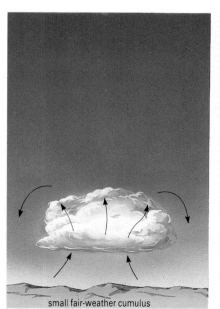

small fair-weather cumulus

cumulus

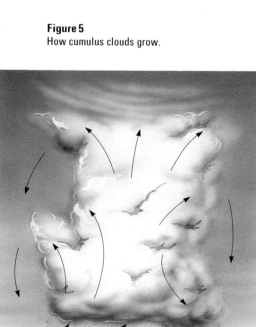

cumulonimbus, with rain

E4 Weather systems

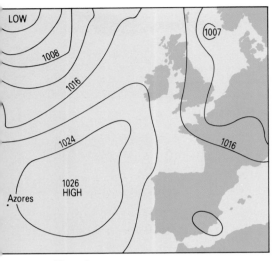

Figure 1
The Azores anticyclone.

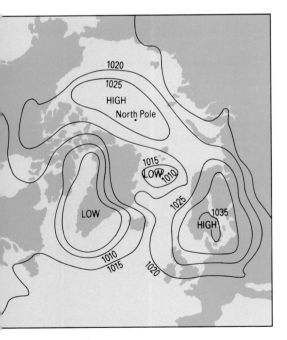

Figure 2
The Polar anticyclone.

This topic started with a look at how changeable the weather in Britain is. Now that you have learned something about the processes that make up 'weather', you can try to see why this is.

Pressure differences in the atmosphere can cause great masses of air to move across the Earth's surface. The temperature and humidity of the air change very slowly as the air masses move, and meteorologists are very interested in these changes.

Sometimes, these masses of air stay more or less in the same place for weeks at a time. For much of the year there is a large high-pressure area (anticyclone) over the Atlantic, somewhere near the islands of the Azores, far to the south-west of Spain (see figure 1). The seas there are quite warm. The air in the anticyclone is moving only a little and it becomes warm and humid. When some of this air mass starts to move north-eastwards towards the British Isles, it brings these warm humid conditions with it. This happens quite often, and people who live on the south-western and southern coasts of Britain are very familiar with the low clouds, mist, fog and drizzle that it brings. This is an example of an air mass in which the properties of the air (that is, its temperature and humidity) stay more or less the same as the air mass travels across the surface of the Earth.

Air masses from other regions of the Earth may be different. For example, there is another anticyclone over the Polar ice-cap (see figure 2). Air in that region will be cooled from below. Being so cold, it can't hold much water vapour, so it becomes very dry as well as quite dense.

Sometimes, in winter and spring, air from the Polar air mass travels across the North Atlantic to reach north-western Britain. As it travels southwards over slightly warmer seas, its lower layers warm up and pick up water vapour. This warming from below is all that is needed to start convection currents going. These carry water vapour upwards, forming cumulus clouds. As a result, heavy showers are likely to occur over much of Britain, especially over the coasts of Scotland and north-west England.

Major changes in our weather occur along the *boundaries* between moving air masses. These boundary regions are called **weather fronts**, or simply fronts. Where moist, warm air from the area of the Azores meets dry, dense and cold Polar air from the ice-cap, one of two types of weather front can be formed.

Warm fronts

A warm front is formed where warm air from the Azores is forced to rise above the denser Polar air (see figure 3). As the warm air rises, it cools,

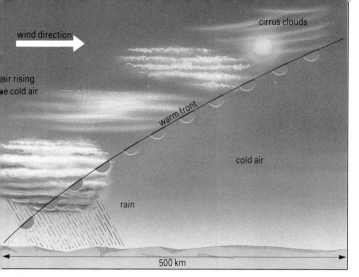

cirrus clouds

wind direction

air rising
...e cold air

warm front

cold air

rain

500 km

Figure 3
A warm front.

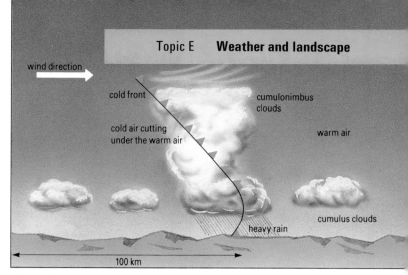

wind direction

cold front

cumulonimbus
clouds

cold air cutting
under the warm air

warm air

cumulus clouds

heavy rain

100 km

Figure 4
A cold front.

and some of its water vapour condenses into droplets, forming thick sheets of cloud which spread over the cooler air below. These cloud sheets may be several thousand kilometres long and a thousand kilometres wide, giving rain for several hours over a large area. Eventually, the warm air replaces all the cold air, the rain stops and the warm front passes on, with a rise in temperature.

Cold fronts

A cold front is formed where Polar air, moving from the north, meets warm air from the Azores and cuts underneath it. The colder air, being more dense, pushes the warmer air away and lifts it from the surface (see figure 4). Convection clouds develop on the front and heavy showers are formed. As the cold front passes, the clouds often clear away rapidly to give blue skies in which small cumulus clouds gradually form.

Fronts are usually found in low-pressure areas or depressions. Their positions are marked on weather maps using special symbols. You can see a warm front and a cold front marked on the weather map in figure 5.

Figure 5
Warm and cold fronts on a weather map.

Figure 6
Giving the weather forecast.

...ather Watch

35

40

Today

Weather forecasting

The type of weather associated with particular patterns of pressure is quite predictable. The difficulty comes in predicting how quickly or how slowly the weather system will move towards Britain, and how much it will have changed when it arrives. The British Isles are a very small area of land compared with the size of the air masses moving over them. Very small changes in the positions of these air masses and in the pressure difference between them can have a large effect on the British weather – it can make the difference between rain or no rain, sunshine or clouds. This is what makes British weather so difficult to predict. Other areas of the world are covered by much more stable pressure systems. In such areas, the weather is very, very predictable.

E5 Water wears away the land

Figure 1
A river system and drainage basin in Arizona.

Figure 2
Professor Adetoye Faniran is a geomorphologist who is interested in the processes of erosion and land-sculpting in tropical areas.

Running water is the most powerful of the agents wearing away and removing the soils and rocks of the Earth's surface. All over the land, wherever it rains, water **erodes** rock and carries off rock particles, eventually depositing them in the sea. This is greatly helped by weathering processes such as frost action and chemical reactions (see Unit B1).

The eroded material is **transported** away to be dumped somewhere else – usually in the sea or a lake. This is called **deposition**. The science of land-shaping by erosion and deposition is called **geomorphology**, which means 'the science of the shape of the Earth'.

You are well aware that the Earth's surface isn't flat! Instead, the Earth's surface is divided into millions of odd-shaped hollows called **drainage basins** (see figure 3). Basins are surrounded by higher ground – perhaps hills, or even mountains. When it rains or snows, the water collects in these basins. It then soaks in, runs over the surface, or evaporates (see figure 4). Which of these it does the most depends upon where the basin is, but generally the water does all three things. The water that does not evaporate collects together to form streams and rivers. Every drainage basin has a river system within it. The river Thames flows in a drainage basin, and so do the Severn, the Spey and so on. Every stream, large or small, is supplied with water that collects in its own basin.

If the rain soaks in, it will become soil moisture. This gradually moves downhill inside the soil until eventually it seeps out again along a river bank. Rivers collect a lot of water in this way.

Some of the rainwater will soak in much more deeply, and helps to make up what is called **groundwater**. This will also move along underground. All streams, rivers and brooks, whatever size they are, get much of their water from beneath the ground surface – often more than they get from **surface flow** during actual rainfall.

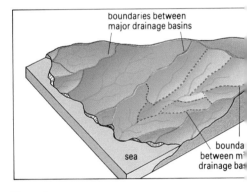

Figure 3
Drainage basins cover most of the land surface of the Earth.

boundaries between major drainage basins

sea

bounda between m drainage ba

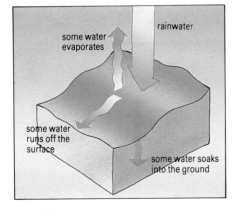

Figure 4
What happens to the water that falls on the land.

rainwater

some water evaporates

some water runs off the surface

some water soaks into the ground

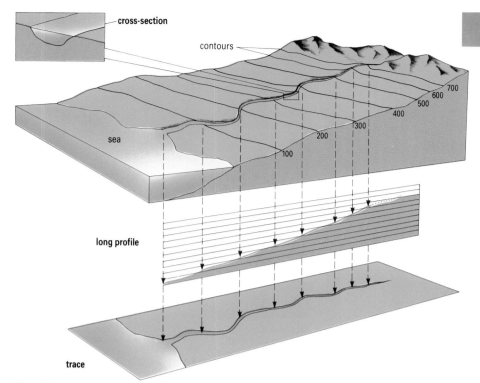

cross-section

contours

700
600
500
400
300
200
100

sea

long profile

trace

Figure 5
Three ways to measure the shape of a stream.

long profile – waterfalls and rapids are smoothed out

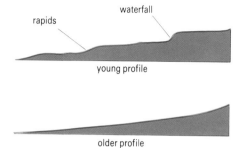

waterfall

rapids

young profile

older profile

trace – sharp bends are smoothed out

young trace

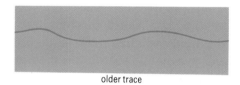

older trace

landscape – hills are worn down

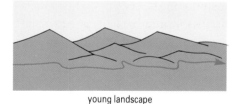

young landscape

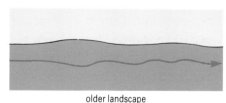

older landscape

Figure 6
How a stream's shape and the landscape change over hundreds of thousands of years.

The water that collects in the bottom of a drainage basin cuts itself a channel. You have seen in Unit C2 that water stored in a reservoir has energy. In the same way, water on the slopes of a drainage basin has energy. As the water moves downhill it rubs against the banks and bed of the channel. Energy is transferred and the channel is eroded to exactly the right size for the water. This scouring action is helped by the gravel, sand and silt carried away by the water.

The shape of the channel is affected by its water and by the rocks over which it is flowing in three ways (see figure 5):

- The width and depth measurements of the channel – these give what is called its **cross-section**.
- The shape of the steam bed from the head to the mouth of the stream – this is called its **long profile**.
- The shape of the stream as seen from above – this is called its **trace**.

Not only does the stream cut a channel of just the right width and depth, it also smooths out its bed. Over thousands and millions of years it gets rid of rough stretches of rapids and waterfalls to produce a smooth profile. It also produces a nicely curved route, seen from above.

We might think that a stream would eventually form a straight route for itself, but in fact it doesn't manage to do that. If it is given a straight channel to begin with, it erodes its banks and becomes curved or **sinuous**. Canal makers have often found this out to their cost when they have tried to dig straight channels for water to flow in.

So the river or stream carries off all the water and solids (**load**) from its drainage basin, and uses the solid particles to help wear away the land surfaces of the Earth.

On these two pages there are twelve terms printed in **bold** type. Write down a meaning for each of them.

71

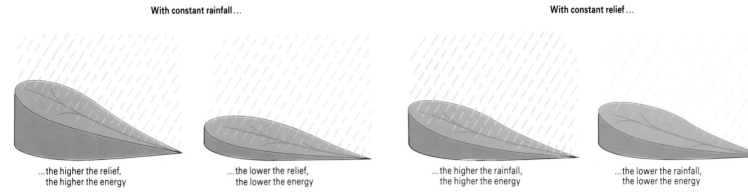

With constant rainfall...

...the higher the relief, the higher the energy

...the lower the relief, the lower the energy

With constant relief...

...the higher the rainfall, the higher the energy

...the lower the rainfall, the lower the energy

Figure 1
The water energy in a drainage basin depends on both the relief and the rainfall.

Streams and river systems in their drainage basins erode more of the Earth's land surface in a year than seas on coasts, glaciers and desert winds put together. The energy needed to do this comes from the water moving downwards through the drainage basins. In Unit C1 you saw that the higher you had to lift something and the heavier it was, the more energy you had to use. It is the same the other way round as well: the more water that runs through a drainage basin in a year and the further it falls, the more energy it can transfer in **denuding** the land.

Apart from the quantity of water and the distance it falls, what other things might affect the amount of erosion that takes place in a drainage basin?

Rain falling on a mountain top will be able to transfer much more energy as it moves downwards in a mountain stream than rain falling near a river mouth. That is why hydroelectric reservoirs are built in highland areas. The trapped water has a good deal of 'highland' energy and travels a long way downwards to reach the turbine system.

Large drainage basins usually have large rivers, and small basins have small rivers. The main river in a drainage basin is fed by **tributaries**, and each tributary is likely to have its own, smaller tributaries, making up a network (see figure 2). If you have a chance, take a map and try walking up a stream. Turn off when you reach a tributary and again when you reach another, smaller, tributary. Go on doing this until you reach the last one, which will probably begin in a spring or in swampy ground.

Usually, most of the water that falls on the drainage basin will soak in. The water moves through the soil and **percolates** down through the cracks and joints of the rock beneath. Eventually, the deeper cracks and pores can hold no more water and the rocks become saturated. This deep water is called **groundwater**. The upper surface of the groundwater is called the

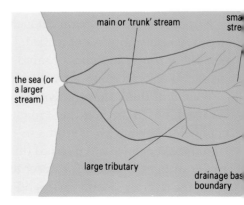

main or 'trunk' stream

sma stre

the sea (or a larger stream)

large tributary

drainage bas boundary

Figure 2
A drainage network.

water table. Water from the groundwater then enters streams and rivers. It can do this by **seeping** out along a stream bank, or it may form a spring.

All streams and rivers, no matter what their size, tend to behave in the same way. In Unit E5 you read about the difficulty canal diggers have in keeping straight banks. Streams always produce a curved (sinuous) channel if they can. Why should that be?

Geomorphologists have many explanations. One of them takes into account the deep **pools** and shallow **riffles** that form in the stream's bed. The stream flows around the edge of a pool, cutting into the bank as it does so. It then crosses over the next riffle to the opposite bank, where it sweeps around the next pool, and so on (see figure 4). But, of course, any tree or boulder can force the stream against the opposite bank, and **undercutting** can occur there to produce a curve.

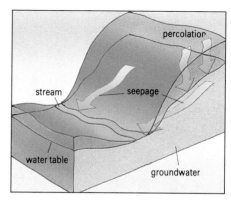

Figure 3
Groundwater is found where the ground is completely saturated with water.

Figure 4
How bends form in a stream.

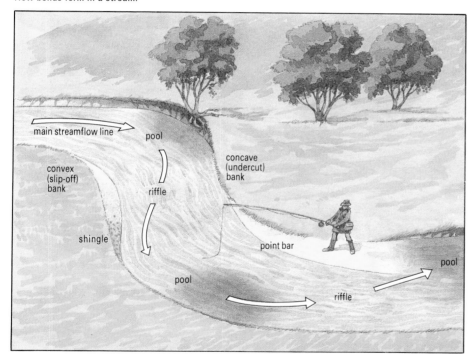

The very slightest tendency for the water to rub against one bank rather than the other soon causes one bank to erode and the other – the **slip-off** bank – to build up. Sometimes the sand and gravel deposited along the inner bank form a **point bar** which juts out into the stream. These make useful platforms for people trying to fish in mid-stream.

Whenever water is flowing downhill in streams and rivers, it is transporting large quantities of eroded material away, out of the drainage basin, to dump it in the sea. It cannot carry the coarser **sediments** far out to sea because the stream water soon loses its energy. So a new land area is built up at the mouth of the river. This is called a **delta**. It is usually made of rich soil and forms a good base for farming (see figure 5).

Figure 5
Ploughing paddy fields in the Ganges delta.

Figure 6
Professor Marie Morisawa has done much research into the processes of rivers.

73

labels on figure: rain clouds; water evaporation from sea; water evaporation from river; river; intake; reservoir; outfall; sewage treatment works; water treatment works; sea; homes and industry; sludge tanker to farms; borehole; groundwater

Every day, millions of litres of water are used in homes, industry and offices. Where does this water come from? Why don't we run out of it?

We cannot use all the water on the Earth. Most of the Earth's water is in the oceans and seas and is too salty. A lot of water is held as ice in polar and mountain areas. The two or three litres a day used by a villager in Africa, or the 160 litres used by a city-dweller in an industrial country, is obtained from rivers, reservoirs or underground water.

This water is continually renewed by rainfall as part of the Earth's great **water cycle**. In this cycle, water on the Earth's surface evaporates, giving water vapour in the air. This forms clouds, and the water returns to the Earth's surface as rain, snow or hail.

Figure 1
This drawing shows parts of the water cycle. It also shows where our water comes from, how water is treated before being supplied to our homes and how sewage is purified after we have used the water.

Some water is taken directly from rivers. River water has to be purified before being fed into water mains because it often contains bacteria or is polluted. Figure 2 shows examples of river pollution.

Another way of obtaining water is by damming a river in a drainage basin. Then, all the streams above the dam pour water into the reservoir. Dammed rivers and reservoirs help with flood control and store water. Reservoir water can be fairly pure, but it usually needs further treatment.

Deep beneath the ground is the massive store of water that we call **groundwater**. This fills all the joints, fissures and pores in the rocks and can be reached by wells or boreholes. In some wells, groundwater will rise up under its own pressure (as in the London area), but normally it has to be pumped up. As the water is taken out, it is replaced by water in the surrounding rock moving towards the borehole. Groundwater is pure so far as bacteria are concerned, but it may contain chemicals dissolved from rocks. Whenever the water is for human use it has to be chemically analysed and suitable purification treatment may need to be carried out.

1 Look carefully at figure 1 and pick out the main parts of the water cycle. Now draw a simpler line diagram of your own to show more clearly the idea of a *cycle*.

2 What types of water pollution can you find in figure 2? Find as many as you can.

Figure 2
This picture shows just some of the ways in which river water may be polluted.

75

THE 'SEA' OF AIR

1 This is a lift pump. It can be used to pump water out of wells.

2 Galileo Galilei, a famous Italian scientist who lived in the sixteenth century found that simple lift pumps could never raise water from wells deeper than about 11 m.

3 Evangelista Torricelli set out to explain why this was. He believed that we live at the bottom of a 'sea' of air and that it was the pressure of this air that pushed the water up the tube of the lift pump.

4 To test his idea, Torricelli filled a tube full of mercury. The tube was sealed at one end. He placed the other end in a bowl containing some more mercury. He found that, no matter how long the tube was, the mercury column was always about 77 cm high.

5 Torricelli said the mercury column was always this height because it was being held up by the pressure of the 'sea' of air on the mercury in the bowl. Mercury is about 14 times as dense as water. So the sea of air will support a column of water 14 times as high – that is, about 11 m high.

6 Blaise Pascal realized that Torricelli's theory meant that a mercury column would be shorter on top of a mountain, because there would be less air pressing down on the bowl of mercury there. It turned out to be just as Pascal predicted.

7 Robert Boyle realized that there could not be any air above the mercury in Torricelli's tubes. He tried pumping the air out of a tube standing in a bowl of mercury. As he expected, the highest he could get the mercury up the tube was about 77 cm.

Is yours dropping too?

11 m.

77 cm

Topic **F** **What is life?**

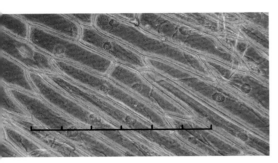

Figure 1
Each division on this scale is 0.1mm wide. How long are the plant cells beside it?

Figure 2
How plants and animals are built up from cells.

In Unit D2 you can read about the chemical elements that make up living things. But there is more to life than that. In this unit you will learn something about the structure of living things. The easiest way to start is by looking at a very thin piece of plant material under a microscope – a piece of onion skin works well. The thin plant skin – called plant **tissue** – looks a bit like a wall built from bricks (see figure 1). All tissues in plants and animals are built up in this way. Each of the separate 'building blocks' is called a **cell**. With a few exceptions, plant and animal cells are very small. If you compare the cells with a scale under your microscope you can measure their size.

How do the cells work together to build up a complete organism – like you, or an oak tree, or a stickleback? Comparing an organism with a building, built of bricks, is in fact quite helpful.

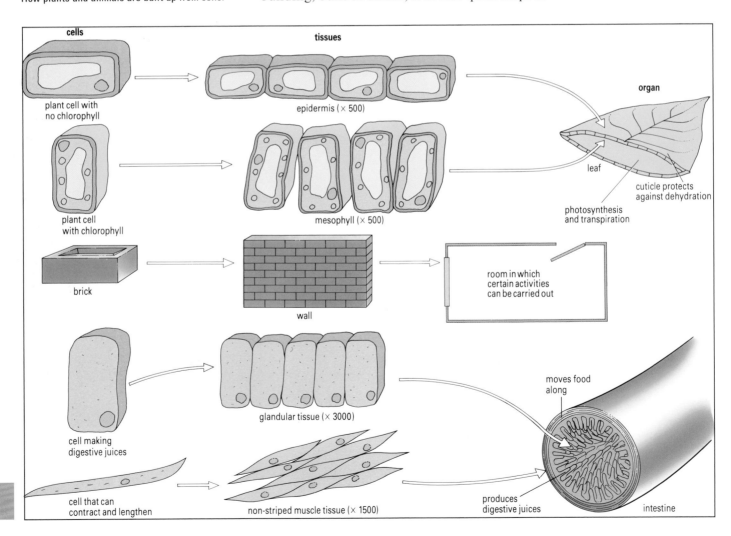

cells

tissues

plant cell with no chlorophyll

epidermis (× 500)

organ

plant cell with chlorophyll

mesophyll (× 500)

leaf

cuticle protects against dehydration

photosynthesis and transpiration

brick

wall

room in which certain activities can be carried out

cell making digestive juices

glandular tissue (× 3000)

moves food along

cell that can contract and lengthen

non-striped muscle tissue (× 1500)

produces digestive juices

intestine

Buildings are some of the commonest things we see in the world around us. Hardly any two buildings are the same, although we can see some 'family likenesses' – you will generally recognize a building as a house, for example, or as a shop. But, however different they look, many buildings have one thing in common – they are all built from bricks. Animals and plants are similar to buildings in this way. No two look quite the same, but they are all built up from various types of 'bricks', which we call cells.

In buildings, bricks can be put together to form walls. In turn, the walls make up rooms, with each room often having a different purpose. In a house, one room may be a kitchen while another may be a bedroom. All these rooms, connected together by doors and corridors, make up the complete building. Organisms are much the same. **Cells** make up **tissues**. These in turn make up **organs**, with each organ having a different job. The organs, connected together, form the complete **organism** (see figure 2).

Figure 3
Using a microscope.

What are cells made of?

Most cells are small, and to see them you have to use a microscope. There are exceptions, though. For example, an egg contains only one cell and yet some eggs (such as birds' eggs) are very large (see figure 4).

Most material from which cells are made is transparent and colourless, so the cell has to be dyed with special stains to make the parts visible. When we examine stained cells under a microscope, we see that plant and animal cells are similar in many ways, but that there are also differences.

All cells are enclosed in a thin skin called the **cell membrane**. Plant cells (but not animal cells) have a thicker layer outside the cell membrane, which is stiffer and made from cellulose. This layer is called the **cell wall**.

Inside cells is a jelly-like substance called **cytoplasm**. The cytoplasm contains apparently empty spaces called **vacuoles**. Plant cells usually have one central vacuole which is very large (see figure 5). Animal cells usually have a larger number of much smaller vacuoles (see figure 6). Plant cells contain the green substance, **chlorophyll**, which helps photosynthesis (see Unit F9).

Nearly all cells have a control centre called the **nucleus** in their cytoplasm. The nucleus is much smaller than the cell, but it too has been found to have a structure. You can learn more about this in Unit F4.

Figure 4
Why is this egg cell so large?

Figure 5
A plant cell.

Figure 6
An animal cell.

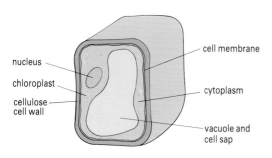

nucleus
chloroplast
cellulose
cell wall
cell membrane
cytoplasm
vacuole and
cell sap

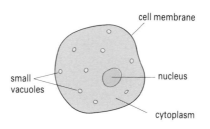

cell membrane
small
vacuoles
nucleus
cytoplasm

1 List a few organs in your body and say what they do.

2 What organs make up your digestive system? (See Unit F6.)

F2 More about cells

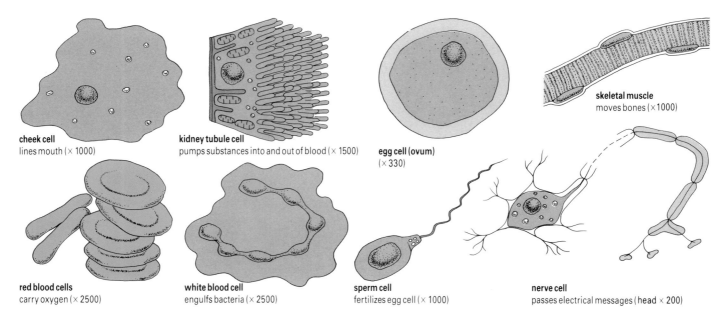

cheek cell
lines mouth (×1000)

kidney tubule cell
pumps substances into and out of blood (×1500)

egg cell (ovum)
(×330)

skeletal muscle
moves bones (×1000)

red blood cells
carry oxygen (×2500)

white blood cell
engulfs bacteria (×2500)

sperm cell
fertilizes egg cell (×1000)

nerve cell
passes electrical messages (head ×200)

Figure 1
Some of the different types of cell that go to make up the human body.

You can see in Unit F1 that there are differences between plant cells and animal cells. There are also differences between one animal cell and another. It all depends on what job the cell has to do.

> **1** Look at the drawings in figure 1. Each different cell is labelled with the job it has to do. See if you can explain, for each cell, how something about it helps it to do its job.

Living cells

Look at the picture of the plant in figure 2a. It looks as though someone has forgotten to water it! Perhaps this has happened to one of your plants when you have been on holiday. Plants that have wilted will often recover if you water them carefully (see figure 2b).

How does water make plants stand upright? To understand this, we shall have to look at a theory about cell membranes and then see how it can explain what happens. Here is the theory: imagine that the cell membrane is not a waterproof skin but in fact has tiny holes in it, a bit like a woollen jersey (see figure 3). You are probably well aware that a thin jersey is not very waterproof – it easily lets the rain through. But if you go out in a snowstorm, you can keep quite dry. The snowflakes are too big to get through the holes in the jersey.

Figure 2

a This plant's owner forgot to water it for several days.

b The same plant after watering.

Figure 3

The holes in a cell membrane are very tiny indeed – just big enough to let through very small molecules, like water molecules, but far too small to let through big molecules. The cytoplasm 'jelly' inside plant cells is full of big molecules – and some water molecules as well. In Unit A3 you learned that molecules are on the move all the time. If there is little water on the outside of a plant cell, the water molecules will soon escape and the plant will wilt (see figure 4a). But if there is a lot of water on the outside, more molecules will be trying to get into the cell than are trying to get out (see figure 4b). So the cell takes up lots of water and gets hard, like a blown-up balloon.

You may be able to test this theory for yourself with an experiment, or perhaps you will see one done.

Figure 4

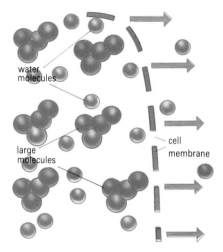

a A plant cell losing water.

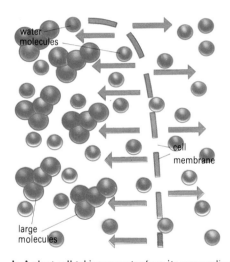

b A plant cell taking up water from its surroundings.

Food for cells

Like all good theories, this one explains something else as well. Cells convert a substance called glucose into carbon dioxide and water (see Unit F7). In doing this they transfer energy from the glucose. Some plant cells can make glucose inside the cell, but all other cells rely on getting it from outside. How does the glucose get into the cell? The cells appear to be completely enclosed by the thin skin we call the cell membrane. You may have guessed the answer. Glucose is also a small molecule – bigger than a water molecule, but still small enough to get through the spaces in the cell membrane. If a cell is surrounded by a solution of water and glucose, then both of these molecules will be able to get into the cell.

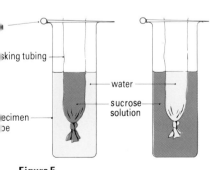

Figure 5
The start of an experiment to investigate water movement. Visking tubing will 'let through' small water molecules but not the larger sucrose molecules. What do you think might happen to the liquid levels?

2 Giving a plant too strong a dose of liquid fertilizer can cause it to wilt. Try to use your theory to explain why this is.

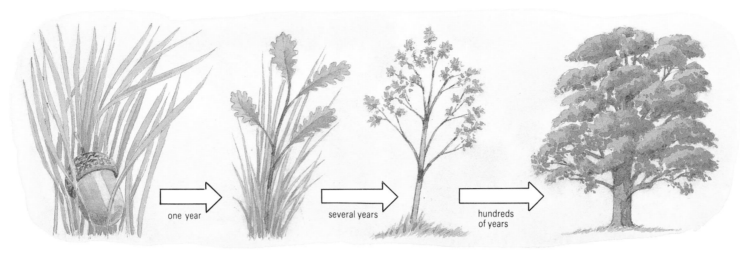

one year

several years

hundreds
of years

Figure 1
The growth of an oak tree.

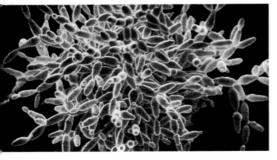

Figure 2
Cell multiplication in yeast.

Figure 3
Dry sultanas compared with wet swollen ones.

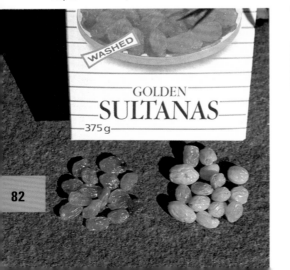

WASHED

GOLDEN
SULTANAS
375g

One of the astonishing things about living things is the way they can increase their own size (see figure 1).

Living things are made up of cells. When they grow they make more cells. Scientists have been able to see this actually taking place (see figure 2). But there is more to it than that. As you grow in height, your legs and arms get longer. The new bone cells are just like the old bone cells, and new muscle cells are just like old ones.

Measuring growth

How do we know that something has grown? It will probably look bigger and weigh more. But you have to be cautious in using weight to measure growth. Have the sultanas in figure 3 grown, for instance?

One way of measuring growth is by finding the increase in *dry* weight over a period of time.

How do you think you could do this for a tray of oat seedlings? Is this a suitable way to measure growth in an animal?

You can follow the growth of an animal by measuring its height or the length of its tail, for example, over a period of time.

In plants, growing takes place from the tips of their stems and roots. This results in the diffuse (spread-out) growth we associate with a plant like an oak tree.

Animals are more compact and grow throughout their bodies – but only for a limited amount of time. Humans, for example, stop growing after fifteen to twenty years. Different parts of your body grow at different rates – for instance, your head grows very fast after birth and reaches 90 per cent of its maximum size at about three years old. Your hands and feet reach their maximum size before the long bones in your arms have reached theirs. This is why many teenagers tend to be clumsy – have you ever wondered what to do with your hands?

Figure 4
Compare the size of the baby's head with the length of her legs. Now do this for your own body.

What affects how big things are?

Adult human beings can vary considerably in their height. If you took any group of adults – those working in a large office, say – you could find their average height. You would find that this average height was much the same, no matter which group of adults you measured. Other organisms (all oak trees or all elephants, say) have different average sizes (see figure 5). What affects the average size of a particular organism?

The average size of human beings depends partly on inheritance, but it depends on other things as well. The sizes of doorways in Tudor houses, antique beds and suits of armour all show that the average height of human beings a few hundred years ago was less than it is today (see figure 6). Scientists have found out that both the rate of growth and the eventual height reached depend to some extent on food and health care. That is why clinics check on the increase in the weight and height of babies.

Some years ago, the Cuban Ministry of Public Health was interested to find out the effects of newly-introduced public-health policies. To check on this, they did a survey of the height and weight of all children and young people in the age range from birth to nineteen. They repeated this with a similar group ten years later. They knew that if their policies were having a beneficial effect it would be shown in the differences between the two surveys. The results of the surveys are shown in figure 7.

Figure 5
Different organisms have different average sizes.

Figure 6
This doorway suggests that humans were once shorter, on average, than they are today.

Figure 7
Explain why these graphs show that the Cuban policy was successful.

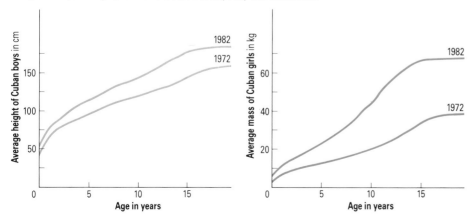

F4 A rose is a rose is a rose ...

Figure 1
Gregor Mendel, the monk who first unravelled the laws of inheritance.

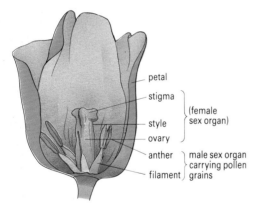

Figure 2
The sex organs of a flowering plant.

petal
stigma
style   (female sex organ)
ovary
anther   male sex organ carrying pollen
filament   grains

1 Plants like the primrose (see figure 3a) are pollinated by insects. What features do their flowers possess that might lure insects?

2 Plants like those in figure 3b are wind pollinated. How do their flowers differ from the insect-pollinated ones?

Looking at family photograph albums can be fun. Have you ever tried to pick out your relations from a group photograph taken a long time ago? Sometimes you can even pick out relations you have never seen, because people from the same family look alike.

Family likenesses seem to be **inherited** – that is, passed on from one generation to the next. It is the same with all living things. If you buy some sweet pea seeds, you know what to expect when the seeds grow. If you get lupins, you suppose that someone put the wrong seeds in the packet!

Research into inheritance started about a hundred years ago in a place now called Brno, in Czechoslovakia. (In those days it was Brünn, in Austria.) Here, in the local monastery, lived a monk named Gregor Mendel (see figure 1). He was a very retiring man with an interest in plants and a passion for mathematics. He used plants to carry out his experiments into inheritance. In order to understand his experiments you need to know how flowering plants reproduce.

Pollination

Flowering plants and many animals reproduce by combining together two special sex cells. This process is called **fertilization**. In animals, the male sex cell is the **sperm** cell and the female sex cell is the **egg** cell. Animals are usually either male, with male sex organs, or female, with female sex organs. Flowering plants, on the other hand, usually possess both male *and* female sex organs (see figure 2). The male sex cells are contained in the pollen grains, while the female sex cells are found at the bottom of the flower head, in the ovary.

Pollen grains from one plant can cross to another flower to bring about fertilization. This process is called **pollination**, and is carried out naturally by the wind or insects.

Figure 3
a Primroses.

b Catkins.

Flowers have a sticky or feathery surface which is attached to the ovary. Pollen sticks to this surface and the male sex cell that it carries is transferred to the female egg cell. A seed develops from the fertilized egg cell, and eventually grows into a new plant.

Mendel had a number of different varieties of pea in his garden. He and his fellow monks pollinated some particularly tall varieties with some very short ones. They then grew new plants from the seeds.

Mendel found that all the new plants were tall. He then decided to grow a new generation of plants using only these new tall ones as parents. The next generation of plants turned out to be a mixture of tall and short ones! Somehow, all the plants were carrying 'instructions' about 'tallness' and 'shortness' from one generation to the next. What could it be that carried this information? Mendel decided that it must be something in the sex cells that combined to form the seed of each new plant.

Cells divide and multiply

New cells are formed by an old cell dividing in half to form two new ones. Scientists have seen this happening, under microscopes (see figure 2 on page 82).

Careful observation and good microscopes have shown scientists that there are some thin thread-like objects, called **chromosomes**, in the nucleus of a cell which also divide up when cells divide (see figure 4). The chromosomes seem to carry all the information about an organism that needs to be passed from one generation to the next. Further experiments have shown that a chromosome is a long coded message. Each bit of the message, responsible for some particular characteristic of the organism, is called a **gene**.

Chromosomes are made from a chemical called DNA (see figure 5). It was not until 1953 that scientists finally unravelled the mystery of how this substance carried the 'message of life' and worked out its chemical structure (see page 98). DNA turns out to be a chemical 'filing cabinet', carrying all the instructions for the life and work of the cell.

Chromosomes are made up of extremely long zipper-like lengths of DNA cleverly folded and packed together. When a cell divides, the DNA unzips, copies itself and then re-forms to give two identical strands – one going to each daughter cell.

Chromosomes themselves are normally paired up in the nucleus of a cell. Sex cells are different from all the other cells in your body – each one has only one chromosome out of every pair found in the other cells. So when sex cells combine, the new individual gets half its 'filing cabinet' of information from one parent and half from the other.

Scientists still do not fully understand how the chromosome filing system works. Perhaps you will become a professional scientist and help to solve this mystery?

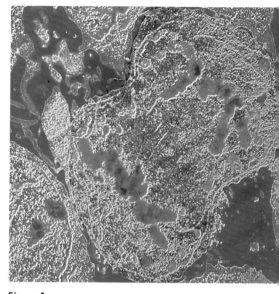

Figure 4
In this picture of a dividing cell, you can see the chromosomes (coloured pink) dividing.

Figure 5
The chemical structure of DNA.

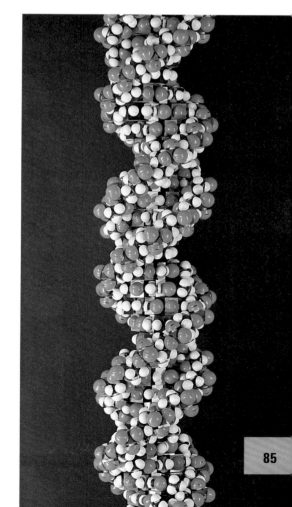

85

F5 Eating to live, or living to eat?

Most humans are interested in food. We sing about it, fight for it, share it with our family and friends, and spend many hours working to gather and prepare it. The food we eat is called our **diet**. Why is food so important to us? Do we all need the same food? Is 'one man's meat another man's poison'? To answer these questions we must know about the things we obtain from food and how our bodies make the best use of their supplies.

Figure 1
Some foods that are rich in proteins.

The food we need

Your diet must supply enough raw material for growth and repair of your body. It must also supply enough energy for living and movement. But how much is 'enough'? An ideal diet must contain three important materials – proteins, carbohydrates and fats.

Proteins are the substances from which cells and tissues are built up. They are made from simpler chemicals called **amino acids**. Every amino acid contains the elements carbon, hydrogen, oxygen and nitrogen. The hundreds of different proteins that go to make up our bodies are built up from only twenty such amino-acid 'building blocks'.

Some proteins form fibres like hair. Others are coiled up. Their shape helps determine the job they can do. A large group of them – called **enzymes** – control chemical processes going on all the time in our bodies.

Carbohydrates is the name given to a family of substances which, along with fats, provide us with energy for living. They are built up from the elements carbon, hydrogen and oxygen. The smallest of the molecules are the sugars, all of which taste sweet. One gram of sugar can provide our bodies with 17 000 J of energy. That's as much energy as you would transfer to a 10 kg bag of potatoes if you lifted it 170 m – almost as high as the tallest office block in London!

Figure 2
Some foods that are rich in carbohydrates.

Figure 3
Some foods that are rich in fats.

Starch is also a carbohydrate. It cannot be used as a food until it is broken down into smaller molecules. Plants make starch to act as an energy reservoir. This energy reservoir is an important source of food for many animals, including humans.

Cellulose is yet another carbohydrate. It is a stiff material used in plants to make cell walls. Cows, as well as many other animals, have bacteria living in their guts that can digest cellulose – that is, turn it into food molecules. This is an important link in the food chain. We cannot digest cellulose ourselves, but we can drink the milk that cows produce. Cellulose does have an important role in our diets even though we cannot digest it. When we eat vegetables, the indigestible cellulose (fibre) passes right through us, performing an important cleaning operation.

Fats contain mainly carbon and hydrogen (and some oxygen) and can provide about 38 000 J of energy from every gram. They are used by organisms as a food reserve. A layer of fat under the skin of mammals helps to keep them warm. It can also act as a shock-absorber – on the soles of the feet and around delicate organs such as the kidneys, for example.

Two other groups of substances are also required to make an organism function properly, but only in very small amounts. These are the **minerals** and the **vitamins**. Some important vitamins and minerals are shown in the table in figure 4.

Is that all we need? Have we left anything out? Water, of course. Water makes up at least 70 per cent of our mass but we are constantly losing it to the environment. To keep healthy we must continually replace it.

Bad management

If you eat more food than your body needs, the extra material is often stored and you 'put on weight'. Carrying this extra mass is hard work. You may become less active, and that makes things worse. You feel low because you think you look awful, and you might eat more to comfort yourself! You can help yourself, though. You can reduce your input (eat less) and increase your output (exercise more). This is called 'dieting'. It should only be carried out with care and under medical supervision.

Eating too little

In many areas of the world, people get too little to eat – they do not get enough protein for growth and repair, or enough carbohydrate for living (see figure 7). Often this shortage of food comes about because of crop failures. When this happens, it is an important task for us all to see that food is supplied from other areas where there is plenty.

Another important problem is to see that people's diets are properly balanced – that is, that they contain the right proportions of all the different foods they need. Unbalanced diets can lead to health problems, just as much as diets that contain too little of everything.

Vitamin A	For healthy eyes
Vitamin B	Helps in obtaining energy from food
Vitamin C	Helps wounds to heal and keeps gums healthy
Vitamin D	For strong teeth and bones
Calcium	For strong teeth and bones
Iodine	Helps in hormone production
Iron	Needed by the blood
Phosphorus	For strong teeth and bones

Figure 4
Some important vitamins and minerals.

Figure 5
A healthy, active human being.

Figure 6
Too much food and too little exercise are one way of making you overweight.

Figure 7
Food being distributed in a relief camp in Ethiopia.

87

F6 Food-processing

The food we eat contains the substances our bodies need for the purposes of living. But it is not in a form that our bodies can use directly. Most food must be physically and chemically broken down into much smaller units before the body can use it. This process of breaking down the food is called **digestion**; it is the job of the **gut**.

Figure 1 shows a diagram of the human gut. As you can see, different sections of it are specialized to deal with different ingredients of your diet.

Figure 1
Different parts of your gut are specialized to do different jobs.

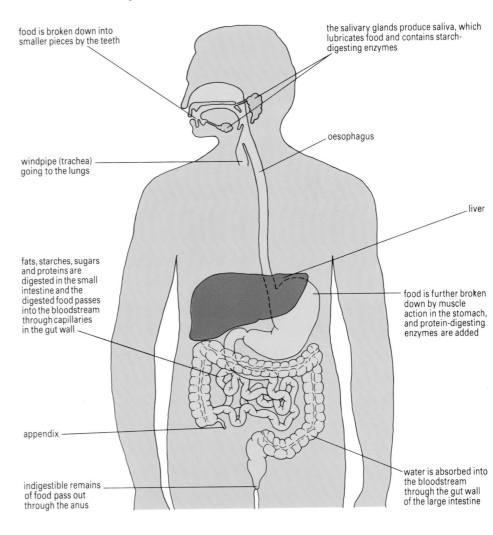

food is broken down into smaller pieces by the teeth

the salivary glands produce saliva, which lubricates food and contains starch-digesting enzymes

windpipe (trachea) going to the lungs

oesophagus

liver

fats, starches, sugars and proteins are digested in the small intestine and the digested food passes into the bloodstream through capillaries in the gut wall

food is further broken down by muscle action in the stomach, and protein-digesting enzymes are added

appendix

indigestible remains of food pass out through the anus

water is absorbed into the bloodstream through the gut wall of the large intestine

Re-processing and storage

Digestion extracts from your food the raw materials your body needs for all its living processes. But your body may not be able to make use of

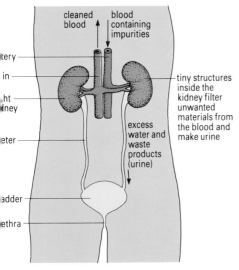

Figure 2
How your kidneys work.

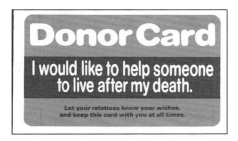

Figure 3
A donor card.

Figure 4
Using a kidney dialysis machine.

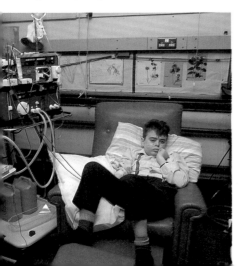

these materials without more chemical processing – and there may be more material there than it needs for its present purposes. Some material can be 'put into store' for later use. It is the function of your liver to help in this process of storage and re-processing.

Once this has been done, the re-processed substances are passed into your bloodstream, to be carried round your body to where they are needed (see Unit F8).

Dealing with waste

The re-processed chemical substances pass into the cells of your body where they perform their useful tasks of growth, repair and releasing energy. Chemical reactions in the cells in turn produce waste products, which also pass into your bloodstream. Your body has to deal with these waste products and the substances it cannot store – if it did not, they would steadily build up in the blood and soon cause a great deal of damage. Cleaning and purifying the blood is the function of the **kidneys** (see figure 2).

The kidneys are very complex and important organs that have to be able to separate out many small molecules. Do you remember how cells could 'sieve' small molecules from large ones, by having spaces that small molecules could pass through? The kidneys have to be 'cleverer' than this, as they have to remove some small molecules, such as urea, but leave others, such as glucose, behind. Your kidneys also control the amount of water circulating in the bloodstream.

The waste liquid from the kidneys collects in the bladder and eventually leaves your body as urine.

In fact, although we normally have two kidneys, one is enough to enable a person to remain in good health and lead a normal life. Failure of both kidneys will lead to death within ten days unless the problem is dealt with. This can be done in a number of different ways.

One thing that can be done is to replace the damaged kidney with a healthy one from another person (called the **donor**). This is referred to as a **transplant** operation. The surgery involved is not difficult, but it is important to match the tissue of the donor to that of the patient as closely as possible. The healthy kidney may be donated by a relative of the sick person, or it may come from someone who has recently died. People who want to donate their organs in this way can sign and carry a donor card like the one shown in figure 3.

If it is not possible to find a suitable kidney donor, a kidney dialysis machine can take over the functions of the failing kidneys. This is used two or three nights a week (see figure 4) and allows life to continue in a reasonably normal way.

In recent years, surgeons have also performed successful liver transplants on people who are suffering from liver failure.

You will probably have realized by now that there are an enormous number of chemical reactions going on inside any living organism. Left to themselves, the raw materials would not naturally react with each other. Two things are needed to make the reaction take place. One of these is a special control substance called an **enzyme**. The other is energy.

Where does the energy come from?

Glucose, which is obtained from food (in the case of animals) or made from simpler chemicals (in the case of plants), is the energy store used by cells.

To transfer this energy, the glucose is broken down into smaller molecules. The way this happens in cells was first worked out by scientists in the 1930s. One of these, Hans Krebs, is pictured in figure 1. A whole series of chemical reactions take place, but a simple shorthand way to write the process is:

$$\text{glucose} + \text{oxygen} \xrightarrow{\text{enzymes}} \text{carbon dioxide} + \text{water} + \begin{array}{c}\text{energy}\\ \text{available for}\\ \text{other purposes}\end{array}$$

These reactions, transferring energy within an organism, are called **respiration**. You probably think of respiration as breathing, but that is not its scientific meaning. Breathing does have a link with respiration – it is the process that enables cells to get the oxygen they need – but that is all.

Respiration produces water and carbon dioxide as by-products. Cells get rid of the carbon dioxide through their cell membranes (remember – these will let small molecules pass through). In the same way, cells can collect up the oxygen they need through their cell membranes. But organisms made of many cells need some way of both distributing oxygen to their cells and getting rid of the waste products to the outside world. Once again, it is the blood system that transports the oxygen and waste products around the body, just as it transports the raw materials.

Organisms take their oxygen directly from the environment in which they live. If they live on land, the organs that provide most animals with the oxygen they need and get rid of the carbon dioxide are the lungs. Animals such as fish, which live in water, have gills which perform a similar function (see figure 3). How should such organs be constructed if they are to perform their function? They will need to have a large surface area and thin tissues separating the air from the blood. You can see a diagram of some lungs in figure 4.

Figure 1
Hans Krebs did a lot of work unravelling the way cells transfer energy.

Figure 2
What happens when you breathe.

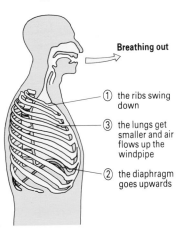

Breathing out

① the ribs swing down

③ the lungs get smaller and air flows up the windpipe

② the diaphragm goes upwards

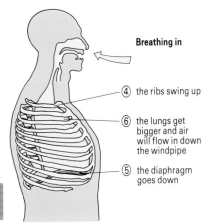

Breathing in

④ the ribs swing up

⑥ the lungs get bigger and air will flow in down the windpipe

⑤ the diaphragm goes down

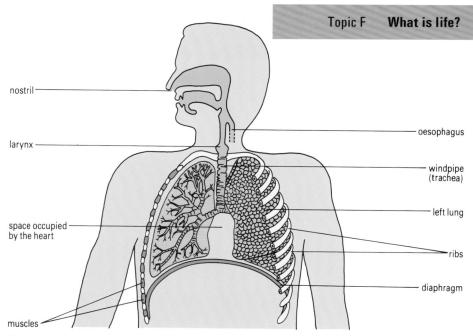

Figure 3
Fish obtain dissolved oxygen from the water they live in through their gills.

Figure 4
The structure of your lungs. (Which one is whole?)

Figure 5
Two uses of fermentation.

a Beer-making.   **b** Bread-making.

The environment the organism lives in may also affect the type of respiration used. Can you think of some places where anaerobic respiration will have to occur?

Respiration without oxygen

Respiration can also take place *without* oxygen, although much less energy is transferred from the glucose. It is called **anaerobic** respiration. This process may occur for a variety of reasons. Muscle cells use it for a short time when there is not enough oxygen available for the amount of energy that is needed. The waste products are carbon dioxide and lactic acid. If lactic acid builds up, you may get a 'stitch' or cramp. Think of situations when this has happened to you.

Yeast, a single-celled fungus, breaks down sugar anaerobically to release energy, carbon dioxide and alcohol. This process (called **fermentation**) has been known for a few thousand years and is still used today in beer- and wine-making (see figure 5a). Yeast is also used in bread-making (see figure 5b). The carbon dioxide produced is used as a 'raising agent'.

How fresh is the air you breathe?

The porous membranes lining your lungs are easily clogged up by dust and other particles in the air. For this reason, small particles are removed from the air you breathe before it reaches your lungs. This cleaning system can break down if there are too many impurities in the air. This can be a serious hazard for people with any sort of lung infection.

Sneezing, often caused by dust in the air we breathe, is part of our natural defences against impurities in the air. It helps prevent our lungs and their filtering system from becoming clogged up.

F8 All together, now!

Figure 1
The London Underground.

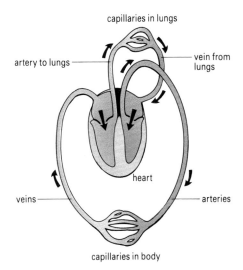

Figure 2

Figure 3
Capillaries branching in a frog's foot.

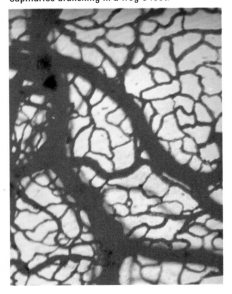

capillaries in lungs

artery to lungs

vein from lungs

heart

veins

arteries

capillaries in body

All large organisms, including humans, need some way of getting substances to the places where they are needed. Simple, one-celled organisms simply rely on diffusion to get chemical substances in and out. Bigger ones cannot do this. In our own bodies, oxygen has to be moved from our lungs to the places it is needed and, similarly, carbon dioxide has to be removed. Food, digested in our gut, also has to be moved to where it is needed and waste products have to be removed. It is the blood system's job to keep everything on the move.

The blood system is a transport system. You can compare it with the London Underground which moves people from place to place (see figure 1). To do this, there have to be carriages for the people to ride in, and engines to drive the carriages. The trains have a route to follow, and there are special places for the passengers to get on and off. You can look at the blood system in the same way. Here, the 'passengers' are the food and gas molecules that have to be moved from place to place. But what about the rest of the system?

Blood and blood vessels

The route the blood follows is made up of tubes, called **arteries**, **veins** and **capillaries** (see figure 2). The capillaries are thin-walled tubes that spread out from arteries (see figure 3), like railway lines often do at a station. It is here that the chemical 'passengers' leave and board the bloodstream.

If you look at some blood under a microscope, you will see that it is largely made up of round blood cells and a thin watery liquid, called **plasma** (see figure 4). Oxygen and some of the carbon dioxide travel 'first class', chemically attached to the blood cells; other substances, which are more soluble, rely on the plasma to carry them along.

Apart from acting as a transport system, blood has another important role. It also protects us against disease. If you examine some blood carefully you will see that as well as the round cells, it also has some irregularly shaped cells, called **white blood cells**. These cells are able to destroy bacteria. This protects our bodies from the many harmful bacteria that we must be picking up all the time.

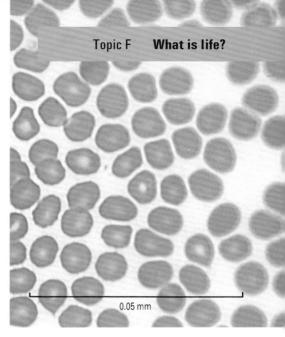

Figure 4
Some red blood cells seen under a microscope.

The heart

The heart is a muscular pump that keeps the blood on the move. If you look at the diagram in figure 5 you will see that it is actually a double pump. One part of it pumps blood around your body; the other part pumps it around your lungs. This makes sure that the blood that returns to the heart is re-oxygenated in the lungs before being sent off on its journey once again.

Plants need a circulatory system, too. Find out how plants move chemical substances from place to place.

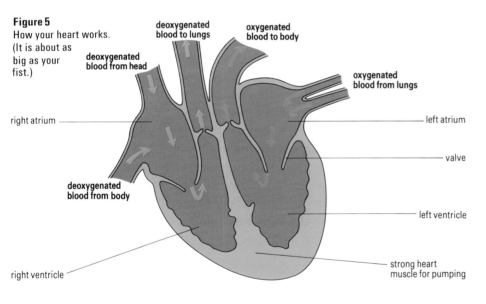

Figure 5
How your heart works. (It is about as big as your fist.)

Figure 6
A nerve cell carrying control signals to a muscle fibre.

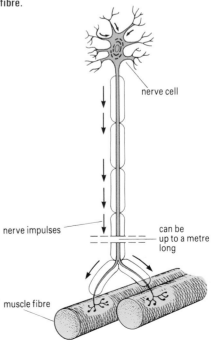

Control

A large transport system like the London Underground cannot be left to run itself. It has to be carefully controlled if it is to operate properly. In the railway system, this is done by linking parts of the system by telephones and signals, all controlled from some central points.

The bodies of large organisms also need a control system. The control is partly carried out by special cells called **nerve cells** (see figure 6), and partly by chemical substances called **hormones**. Signals sent by this system keep our hearts beating, our lungs operating, and many, many more things happening. Our brains are largely, but not entirely, in control of the system.

F9 Where it all begins

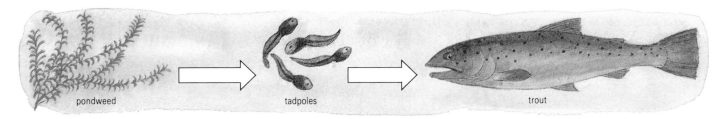

pondweed   tadpoles   trout

Figure 1
A simple food chain.

Figure 2
Van Helmont's experiment.

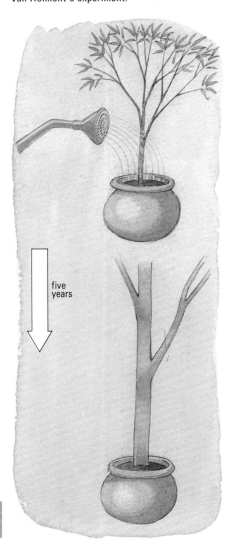

five years

What did you eat yesterday? Chips? Salad? Rice? Fish? Where did your food come from? If it was an animal, like a fish, where did the fish get its food? In Unit B5 you can see that all living things are part of a food chain and that all food chains start with plants (see figure 1). So everything you eat comes, directly or indirectly, from plants.

You need food to provide your body with its energy store and the raw materials for living and growing. Plants also need energy and raw materials for the same purposes. Where does it all come from?

Early in the seventeenth century, a Belgian physician, Johann Baptista van Helmont, carried out a famous experiment. He carefully dried and weighed the soil in a large tub and then planted a small willow tree in it (see figure 2). The willow tree had a mass of just over 2 kg. For five years he carefully watered the tree, but otherwise he gave it nothing. At the end of that time he dried the soil in the tub and reweighed it. After drying it to a constant mass, he found that the mass of the soil was almost exactly the same as when he started the experiment – but the tree now weighed almost 75 kg! Where had all the substances that now made up the tree come from? Van Helmont thought they must all have come from the water he had given the tree during the past five years.

This experiment puzzled a number of scientists. Robert Boyle, Antoine Lavoisier and Joseph Priestley did more experiments to find out where plants got their raw materials from. Robert Boyle realized that water alone could not have provided all the materials. At first, scientists thought that plants used substances dissolved in water. Then Lavoisier suggested that the plants might be using the air as well as water. During the nineteenth century, many other scientists carried out more experiments to test out this idea. You may be able to try some of them for yourself. These experiments have shown that plants are capable of combining carbon dioxide, from the air, with water to make glucose. Glucose is then used by the plants for their purposes of living and growing. To make glucose, plants need light, enzymes and chlorophyll. It is chlorophyll that gives the green colour to plants. This energy-storing reaction is called **photosynthesis** (see figure 3). Many chemical reactions are involved, but the overall process can be written as:

$$\text{carbon dioxide} + \text{water} + \text{energy} \xrightarrow{\text{enzymes and chlorophyll}} \text{glucose} + \text{oxygen}$$

What do you notice about this word equation? Look back at Unit F7. You should see that it is almost the reverse of the one for respiration.

Once the glucose has been formed, plants may use it to make starch (which is an energy store) or convert it into cellulose and protein for growth. So most of a plant is built up from the material produced by photosynthesis.

The carbon cycle

All living things depend on the elements used in photosynthesis – carbon, hydrogen and oxygen. These elements, together with nitrogen, make up most of the substances from which living things are made (see Unit D2). What happens to these materials? If plants have been taking carbon dioxide out of the atmosphere for hundreds of millions of years, why haven't we run out of it?

Directly or indirectly, all other living things depend on plants for food. When food is broken down in an organism to release energy, the carbon dioxide is returned to the atmosphere. So the carbon that is taken up by plants in growing is returned to the atmosphere in respiration. Both plants and animals respire, so both help to return the carbon dioxide.

This is a part of the **carbon cycle**. Instead of being used up, carbon is continually recycled and used again and again by living things. Many plants and animals do not get eaten, but die and decay. The process of decay also releases carbon which eventually finds its way back to the atmosphere.

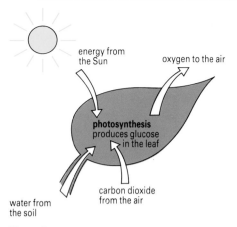

Figure 3
The changes taking place during photosynthesis.

Figure 4
The carbon cycle.

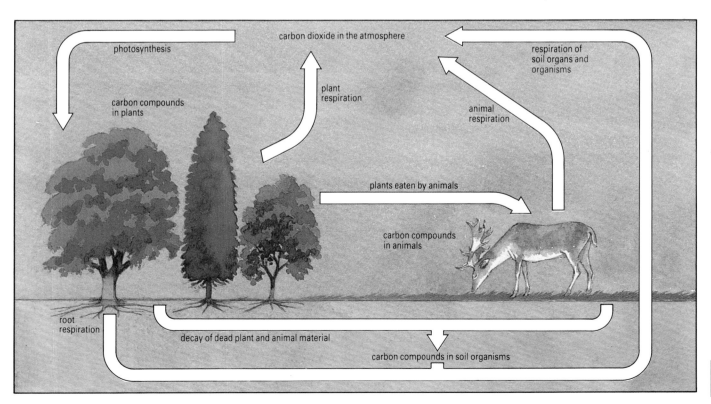

F10 Food for the world

a French bean plants.

b These lumps on their roots are the home of bacteria that can live on nitrogen in the air.

Figure 2
Lightning helps to change atmospheric nitrogen into a form plants can use.

Photosynthesis in plants combines carbon dioxide from the air with water from the soil to make glucose. Glucose gives plants an energy store and the main raw material they need for growth. But plants also contain other complex substances which have a variety of jobs to do. Photosynthesis cannot provide all the elements needed to make these substances. One other important element needed by all living things is nitrogen. Getting sufficient nitrogen is a special problem for plants. Let us see why this is so.

There is a world-wide store of the carbon dioxide and water that photosynthesis depends on. This store is the atmosphere and the oceans. Water enters the atmosphere as water vapour. Carbon dioxide, along with water vapour, is swirled and mixed so that it is available anywhere in the world. Unless there is a drought, photosynthesis can take place almost anywhere on Earth. You might think that, similarly, there should be no problem over the supply of nitrogen – after all, nearly 80 per cent of the atmosphere is nitrogen! But plants cannot make direct use of the nitrogen from the atmosphere, because it is a much less reactive gas than oxygen. Instead, they rely on nitrogen being available, combined with other elements, in the soil.

The cleverness of the bean plant

One family of plants has a particularly clever way of dealing with the 'nitrogen problem'. Their roots are the home for a special sort of bacteria which take nitrogen from the atmosphere as part of their living processes. This nitrogen is then made available to the plants in a form they can use. Crops such as peas and beans (see figure 1), as well as plants like clover, are all members of this family. These plants are called **legumes**.

The nitrogen cycle

The Earth's stock of nitrogen, like its stocks of all other elements, is neither increasing nor decreasing. Like carbon and oxygen, nitrogen must be recycled if plants and animals are to continue to be able to make use of it. The recycling of nitrogen is called the **nitrogen cycle** (see figure 3). Plants take in nitrogen from the soil. This nitrogen passes on to animals in their food. Nitrogen returns to the soil in two main ways – from the decay of plants and animals when they die, and from the waste material excreted by animals. Animal waste is rich in nitrogen compounds. Bacteria are essential to the recycling process. By their activities, they produce the nitrogen compounds that plants can use.

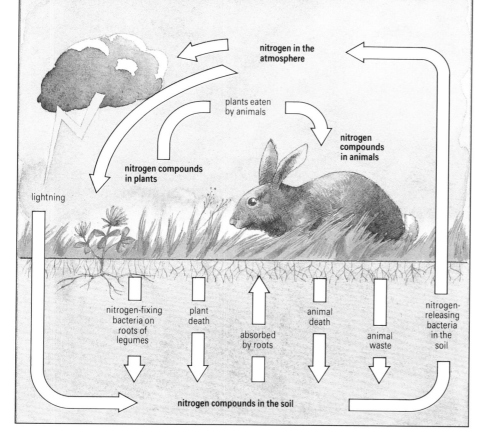

Figure 3
The nitrogen cycle.

Figure 4
Townshend's four-year crop-rotation programme.

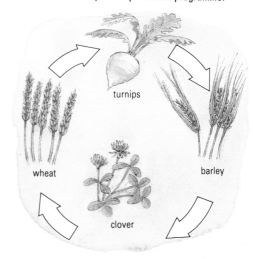

Growing crops

Crops are plants grown specially for food. When they are harvested, they will take nitrogen away from the soil in which they were growing. In the eighteenth century, Charles Townshend solved this problem by introducing a new system of 'crop rotation' (see figure 4). Over a four-year period he grew wheat, roots (such as turnips), barley and clover in turn.

Which crop helped to restore the nitrogen to the soil?

Improving crop production

Can you see any disadvantages in Townshend's four-year crop-rotation programme? One is that a field only produces crops in three years out of four. There are other disadvantages as well – intensive crop production may still take more nitrogen from the soil than any other crop can replace. To overcome these difficulties we have to give the nitrogen cycle some help. We can do this in two ways. The first is to spread animal waste over fields. This waste is usually referred to as **farmyard manure**, as it is readily available from the animals on a farm. Such waste is rich in nitrogen. The second way is to make chemical compounds of nitrogen that plants can use. These are called **artificial fertilizers**. Many artificial fertilizers are made from ammonia, which is manufactured from hydrogen and nitrogen. So artificial fertilizers do what most plants cannot do – take nitrogen from the air and make it available to plants. Artificial fertilizers also make up the losses of other elements, such as potassium and phosphorus, from the soil.

Figure 5
Farmyard manure is very rich in nitrogen.

97

THE INHERITANCE MOLECULE

In the 1950s, two groups of scientists studied DNA for different reasons

nucleus

1 When organisms reproduce, the offspring are like their parents. 'Information' about an organism is carried from one generation to the next one by genes.

1 DNA is a complex chemical found in the nucleus of all cells.

How are the atoms that make up DNA fitted together?

But what are genes?

2 Maurice Wilkins makes DNA fibres. X-ray diffraction pictures show that DNA may have a regular crystalline structure.

What shapes have we got?

2 Francis Crick and James Watson believe that the answer to this problem lies in the structure of DNA.

3 A brilliant experimental scientist, Rosalind Franklin joins Wilkins to t to get better X-ray pictures, in order unravel the structure of DNA.

A   T
G   C

There's phosphates, sugars and 4 bases A, C, G and T tied up somehow!

4 Rosalind Franklin refuses to cooperate with Crick and Watson, believing their model-building is pure guess-work.

They make a helix!

Sheer Child's play!

They're just guessing The phosphates can't b inside the molecule.

A form of DNA

3 Crick and Watson try to build a model of DNA that will be able to make copies of itself. They have little information to go on but believe it will have the shape of a helix.

4 Their first model is a failure.

5 Meanwhile she concentrates on compiling data on one form (the of DNA.

5 Crick and Watson rethink their model, concentrating on the way it must behave if genes are part of DNA.

A helix would give a cross pattern. I can't see one on the 'A' form of DNA

But what a & the 'B' for

B form DNA

With bases on the inside it makes 2 interlocking spirals

And it can remake itself!

It works!

6 Collecting together ideas from a variety of other work, they realize that the structure of DNA is a double helix, linked together by just four different chemical structures called 'bases'. These four bases are the 'letters' of the genetic code.

6 Rosalind Franklin at last turns to the B-form of DNA and analyses its structure on the basis of her X-ray p She too realizes it is a double helix. Wilkins' and her careful experimenta confirm the model Crick and Watson have built.

GROWTH

Topic G Communication

G1 Range-finding

Figure 1
How can a bat catch an insect when it is completely dark? How does an automatic camera know where to focus when it is taking a picture? How can a ship know the depth of water in which it is sailing? How does a control tower know where the aircraft are when the skies are cloudy?

Figure 2
A radar scanner for controlling air traffic at Heathrow airport.

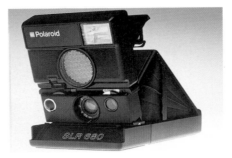

Figure 1 shows several situations where there is a need to find the position of something that can't be seen.

You may know that airport control towers use radio waves for this purpose. Bats, ships and some modern cameras use sound to find out where things are. Using radio waves to find the position of aircraft is called **radar**. Using sound to find the position of things is called **sonar**. Both work by using echoes.

You probably hear echoes every day. A bathroom can be a good place for echoes. Sounds that you make bounce off the walls around the room and get back to your ears. When sound is bouncing off the walls like this, we say that it is being **reflected**. In the bathroom you hear many echoes from different walls, and they make your voice sound 'bigger'. That is why it is so much fun to sing in the bath.

Sometimes when we are outside, we hear just one echo from a single wall. Sonar works by sending out a sound and listening for the echo that bounces off objects. The further away an object is, the longer it takes for an echo from it to get back. Measuring distances by this method is called **range-finding**.

Bats use sonar to find the insects they eat. They give out a 'chirp' of sound that is too high for humans to hear. As the bats listen to the echoes of the chirp, they can find out what is around them (see figure 3).

Ships use sonar to find out how deep the water is that they are sailing in. They send out a 'beep' through the water and time how long it takes to bounce back from the sea bed (see figure 4).

a 'chirp' of sound from the bat...

...bounces off the insect

Figure 3

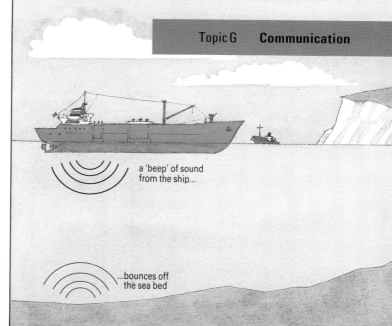

a 'beep' of sound from the ship...

...bounces off the sea bed

Figure 4

Suppose an insect is flying 3 metres in front of a bat. Sound travels at a speed of about 300 metres per second. How long would it take for an echo to return to the bat after bouncing off the insect? How long would it be from the moment the bat made a sound to the moment it heard the echo?

Reverberation

Echoes are not always useful. In a hall in which music is being played, they can muddle up the sound. Some things – like hard ceilings, brick walls and stone floors – reflect sound very well. Any sound you make in an empty building which has these will take a long time to die away as it bounces from one surface to another. Bathrooms behave like this too.

When sound bounces around a room, it is said to **reverberate**. If a sound takes a long time to die away, the room is said to have a long **reverberation time**. Soft coverings on the walls, floors and ceiling of a room and soft furniture in it will absorb sound instead of reflecting it. This causes any sound to die away quickly. Such rooms have short reverberation times.

The reverberation time of the Royal Albert Hall (a concert hall in London) used to be so long that echoes muddled up the music. Sound-absorbing plates are now hung from the ceiling to absorb sound and reduce the reverberation time of the hall.

It is important not to make reverberation times too short, either. Short reverberation times can make musical sounds dull and uninteresting. Some halls, such as the one shown in figure 6, have had their reverberation times artificially increased. To do this, microphones and loudspeakers have been installed to create artificial echoes and so increase the reverberation time.

Figure 5
Inside the Royal Albert Hall.

Figure 6
Some of the microphones used to increase the reverberation time in the Central Hall of York University.

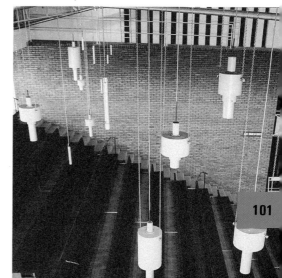

101

Figure 1

Figure 2
Time-exposure of a vibrating guitar string.

Figure 3
We cannot *see* the cone moving at high frequencies, but it will throw sand particles around all the same.

All the things in figure 1 make sounds. What else do they have in common? With a road-drill or a chirping locust, it is possible to *see* that the sound is made by something moving. When a guitar makes a noise, you know that the string has been plucked. If you touch a guitar string that is making a sound, you can *feel* it moving. The photograph in figure 2 shows how it moves.

You can find out some more things about sound by using a **signal generator** attached to a loudspeaker. The signal generator makes the loudspeaker cone move up and down. This is called **vibrating** or **oscillating**.

If you watch a loudspeaker cone when it is moving slowly, you can see that the cone moves up and down until it is back in the position it started from. This complete up-and-down motion, finishing at the original position, is called one **oscillation** (see figure 4).

When the loudspeaker cone is moving slowly, it makes very few oscillations every second. If the loudspeaker cone moves more quickly, it can complete more oscillations in a second. We use the word **frequency** to describe how many oscillations the loudspeaker cone makes in one second.

Frequencies are measured using a unit called the **hertz**. If a loudspeaker cone makes 300 oscillations in a second, we say that its frequency is 300 hertz (written Hz for short).

As the loudspeaker cone is made to move faster and faster, it starts to produce a noise. This happens when the frequency is high enough – between 20 Hz and 30 Hz. At this frequency you cannot follow the vibrations of the loudspeaker with your eyes. But if you touch it with your fingers you can feel that it is moving.

As the frequency of the cone's movement gets higher, the pitch of the note it makes gets higher. High notes are produced from vibrations of high frequencies. Eventually, as the frequency becomes very high, there comes a point when you cannot hear any sound from the loudspeaker any more. This happens at a frequency of about 20 000 Hz when you are young, but at lower frequencies as you get older.

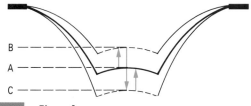

Figure 4
In one complete oscillation, the loudspeaker cone moves from A to B to C and back to A.

What makes loud sounds loud?

The signal generator has an output control on it, rather like the volume control on an amplifier. If you increase the output from the signal generator, the sound becomes louder. What happens to the loudspeaker?

Once again, you can find out if you look at the loudspeaker at low frequencies. If you get the loudspeaker to oscillate at about 2 Hz and then change the output control, you can see what effect this has on the loudspeaker cone. When the output from the signal generator is low, the cone does not move very far up and down. When the output is high, the cone travels much further. Quiet sounds come from small vibrations; loud sounds come from big ones.

How does sound travel?

The sound starts out from the loudspeaker cone. But how does it get to your ears? You know from the work on range-finding (Unit G1) that sound can travel through air and through water. But what if there is *nothing* between the source of the sound and your ears? We can find out by putting a bell in a jar and taking the air out of the jar (see figure 6). Even though you can *see* the bell ringing, you cannot *hear* it if the air has been taken out of the jar. Sound cannot travel through a vacuum.

Sound vibrations travel through the air in the same way as vibrations travel along a Slinky spring. The air particles come together and move apart just like the coils on the spring in figure 7.

Figure 5
The unit of frequency is named after Heinrich Hertz, who carried out some of the first experiments on radio waves.

Figure 6
You may be shown this experiment with a bell in a vacuum.

Figure 7
Sound travels through the air in the same way as these vibrations travel along a spring.

When you go swimming, can you hear sounds under water? Try to test this out next time you are in a swimming pool.

G3 The ear and hearing

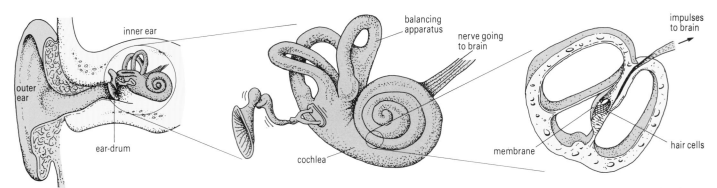

inner ear

outer ear

ear-drum

sound collected by the outer ear hits the ear-drum

balancing apparatus

nerve going to brain

cochlea

the bones of the middle ear transmit the vibrations to the fluid inside the cochlea

impulses to brain

membrane

hair cells

sensitive cells inside the cochlea pick up the vibrations and send nerve impulses to the brain

Figure 1
The journey of a sound wave through the ear.

Figure 2
The large outer ear structure of the bat helps it to pick up faint sounds.

Figure 3
Some frogs find their mates by making special calls.

104

How does sound travel through the air? If you look at Unit G2 you will see that we think it travels in the same way as pulses travel along a Slinky spring. Backwards-and-forwards movements of the air will cause anything it hits to move backwards and forwards in the same way. This is how we hear.

It is difficult to examine the ear of an animal as it is made of bone. Scientists who have done it have found out that the structure of the ear is as shown in figure 1. The air vibrations produced by a sound fall on a sheet of skin and muscle, called the **ear-drum**. This picks up the vibrations and passes them to the **inner ear**.

The inner ear is quite a complicated structure, part of which is concerned with our sense of balance. The 'hearing' part consists of a coiled tube called the **cochlea**. Within the cochlea is a carpet of tiny fibres. It is these that respond to the sound vibrations passing into the ear. Somehow or other (and scientists are still not entirely sure how), different parts of this fibre carpet respond to sounds of different frequencies. Nerve impulses from the fibres pass to the brain, which is able to 'hear' sounds and pick out the different frequencies. There is a limit to the range of frequencies we can hear (see Unit G2). No human can hear sounds much higher than 20 000 Hz, but many animals can do better. Bats, for example, send out and hear sounds as high as 150 000 Hz (see figure 2).

Finding out where sounds come from

Sound sense is very important to many animals. Sound can warn an animal of danger, alert it to the presence of prey, or be a courtship call during the mating season (see figure 3). To make use of such sounds, an animal not only has to distinguish one sound from another, but also to know where it comes from.

The outer structure of the ear, called the **pinna** (the part you wash!), is funnel-shaped and enables an animal to collect the energy from even the feeblest sounds. Many animals can move their ears to pick up the sound. You have probably seen dogs 'pricking up their ears' when they hear a faint sound.

We, and other animals, need two ears to locate sounds. The strength of a sound arriving at one ear is slightly different from its strength at the other. The difference depends on exactly where the sound is coming from. This may be one of the ways that the brain can locate a sound source. There may be others – for example, there is a time-delay between a sound pulse arriving at one ear and at the other.

Figure 4
This dog has heard a faint sound.

Loudness

Ears are very sensitive to sound. The eye can control the amount of light it receives (see Unit G6), but ears cannot control the amount of sound reaching the ear-drum.

Unit G2 describes an experiment which shows that the bigger the vibration of a loudspeaker, the louder the sound it produces. Loud sounds make the ear-drum vibrate with bigger movements than soft sounds do.

The loudness of a sound is measured in units called **decibels** (dB). Scientists have constructed a loudness scale, starting with 0 for the faintest sound we can normally hear. You can see a loudness scale in figure 5.

Very loud sounds can actually cause pain. If your ear has to cope with very loud sounds for long, your hearing can be permanently damaged. Many doctors are very concerned that some music may be so loud that people listening to it for any length of time may be damaging their hearing. Particular care should be taken over the use of headphones – even small cassette-players can give dangerously high sound levels (see figure 6). People who have to work in noisy environments now have to wear ear-muffs to protect their hearing.

jet aircraft taking off	130 dB
road-drill 1 m away	120 dB
rock group	110 dB
baby crying loudly	100 dB
inside a noisy truck	90 dB
loud radio	80 dB
inside a large shop	70 dB
telephone conversation	60 dB
normal conversation	50 dB
birds singing	40 dB
library reading room	30 dB
soft whisper	20 dB
falling leaf	10 dB
threshold of hearing	0 dB

VERY VERY LOUD

very very quiet

Figure 5
Loudness scale.

Figure 6
Is it too loud?

105

G4 Reflection

Figure 1
In what way do these reflectors do similar jobs?

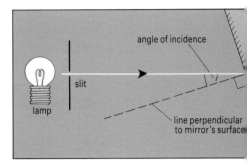

Figure 2
The ray striking the mirror is called the **incident** ray. The angle between the incident ray and the perpendicular is called the **angle of incidence**, *i*.

The bicycle reflector and the laser reflector in figure 1 are both designed to send light back in the same direction as it came from.

When light falls on a rough surface it is scattered in all directions. Smooth surfaces, such as mirrors, reflect light in a regular way. If we know at what angle the ray hits the mirror, we can predict at what angle the ray will leave it.

Figures 2 and 3 show how the angles at which a light ray strikes and bounces off a mirror are measured.

Experiments with regular reflectors show that the angle of incidence is equal to the angle of reflection. This is called the **law of reflection**.

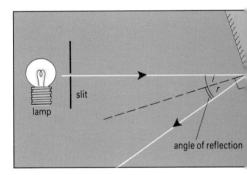

Figure 3
The ray that bounces off the mirror is called the **reflected** ray. The angle between the reflected ray and the perpendicular is called the **angle of reflection**, *r*.

Where is the image in a mirror?

When you look into a mirror, you see something in the mirror that looks like yourself. That is called an **image**. Where is this image? If you put your hand on the surface of the mirror, you can see that the image is behind your hand, so it is not on the surface of the mirror. Small children and animals are often fooled into believing that there is something behind the mirror and they will look behind to try to find it.

Why does the image seem to be behind the mirror? How does your brain work out where an image is?

If you look at the three spreading-out rays of light in figure 4, you will see that the lamp is where the three rays meet. Your brain can work out where an object is by tracing the rays of light backwards.

Cover up figure 6 and look at figure 5. Where does your brain think the rays of light are coming from? Copy the diagram and mark on it where the light seems to be coming from. Now look at figure 6. The rays of light have been reflected by a mirror. The point where the rays seem to come from is the point where you would see an image of the lamp in the mirror.

Figure 4
Your brain can work out where the lamp is because the rays are spreading out from the lamp.

Getting a ray to go back to where it started

This unit began by looking at two devices that sent rays back to where they started from. Can we use mirrors to make an arrangement that will do this?

Suppose there are two mirrors at right angles. What will happen to a ray that hits one mirror and then the other? It doesn't matter at what angle it hits the mirror, it will always bounce back in the same direction as it came from (see figure 7).

A similar arrangement, with *three* mirrors at right angles, is used for the bicycle and laser reflectors in figure 1. Three mirrors are used, so that *any* ray that hits the arrangement will be reflected back in the same direction as it arrived. This arrangement is called a **corner reflector** because it is like the corner of a box. The corner reflector sends a ray straight back to where it came from.

The laser-beam reflector was left on the surface of the Moon when the *Apollo 14* spacecraft landed there. This reflector helps scientists on the Earth to measure the distance between the Earth and the Moon very accurately. A laser beam is pointed at the Moon and a very powerful telescope is used to pick up the reflection. Electronic timing is used to measure how long it is between when the laser light leaves the Earth and when it arrives back from the Moon.

This method of measuring the distance between the Earth and the Moon uses light reflections in the same way as sound reflections are used to measure the depth of water under a ship (see Unit G1).

In one experiment, it took 2.7 seconds for light to get from the Earth to the Moon and back. Light travels at 300 000 kilometres per second. How far away does this mean the Moon is from the Earth?

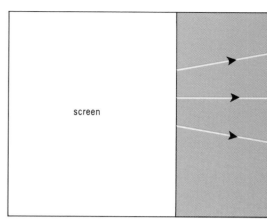

Figure 5
Where do you think the light is coming from?

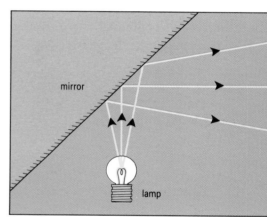

Figure 6
There is a mirror behind the screen, and the light rays seem to be coming from behind it.

Figure 7
A two-dimensional corner reflector.

Figure 8
Measuring the distance to the Moon. Pulses of laser light are sent out from the Earth and a special clock times how long it takes for the pulses to travel to the Moon and back.

about 400 000 km

pulsed laser beam

reflector on Moon

telescope on Earth

G5 Using lenses

A pinhole camera can make a picture of any well-lit scene on a screen at the back of the camera. We refer to the original scene as the **object** and its picture on the back of the camera as its **image**. Pinhole cameras are easy to make but the image is very faint. If you want to see the image you need to stop stray light getting onto the screen. If you want to take a photograph, you need a very long exposure time. How can the camera be improved to let more light through?

If you make the pinhole in the camera bigger, the image gets brighter but more blurred. With a large hole, much more light gets to the screen. But the light from each point on the object produces a *patch* of light on the screen. The patches of light from all the different parts of the object overlap and the image is no longer sharp (see figure 2b).

Figure 1
Pinhole camera.

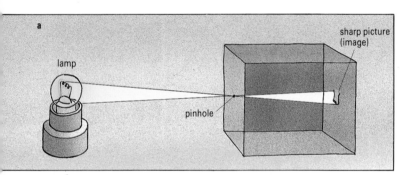

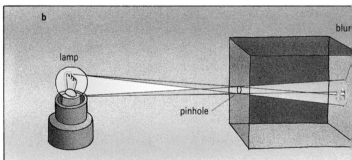

If you get a lens of the right shape and put it in front of the large hole, a sharp image will be formed on the screen once more. The lens catches all the light rays from one point on the object and bends them so that they all pass through another point. This is the place where the image is (see figure 2c). The sort of lens that bends light like this is called a **converging** lens.

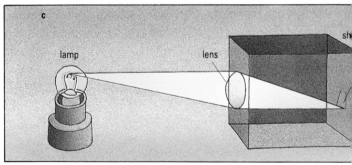

Figure 2
a With a small hole in the pinhole camera, light from one point on an object lands at one small point on the screen.
b With a large hole, light from one point on an object lands in several different places, and the image is blurred.
c Using a lens, all the light passing through the large hole is bent to form an image.

Focusing

Suppose your converging lens forms an image of a distant object close to the lens (see figure 3a). If you move the lens closer to the object, the image is formed further away (see figure 3b). If you want to get sharp images of objects at different distances from the camera, you will need some way of changing the distance between the lens and the film. This adjustment is called **focusing** the camera. On some cameras the photographer has to do this; in others, the movement of the lens for focusing is done automatically.

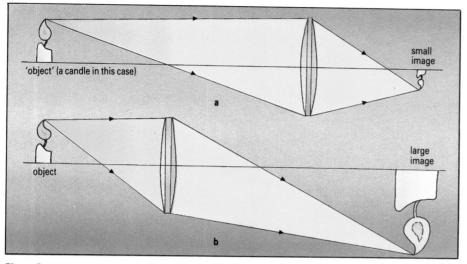

Figure 3
a When the object is a long way from the lens, the image is close to the lens.
b When the object is close to the lens, the image is further from the lens.

1 Some inexpensive cameras cannot be focused but still give acceptable pictures. Find out why this is.

Aperture, shutter speed and exposure

Focusing isn't the only adjustment you have to make to a camera when you take a picture. The film needs just the right amount of light falling on it to take a good picture. This is called the **exposure**. There are two ways of controlling the total amount of light that gets onto the film. One way is with the **aperture**. Behind the lens is a hole whose size can be varied by using the aperture control. If the aperture is small, then very little light will get through. If the aperture is large, then much more light will get through.

The other way to control the exposure is with the **shutter**. If the shutter speed is high, the shutter is only open for a short time, and the amount of light that gets in is small. If the shutter speed is slow, the shutter is open for a long time and the amount of light that gets in is large.

Nowadays, many cameras control the aperture and the shutter speed automatically.

Slide-projectors

With a camera we have to make a small image of a large object. With a projector we want to get a *larger* image of a *small* object (the slide). We can make a large image by placing the object close to the lens. This is what happens in a slide-projector.

2 Slide-projectors made for the home are no use in large halls, where the projector is usually right at the back. The image would be far too big! What differences are there between a home slide-projector and one for use in a large hall?

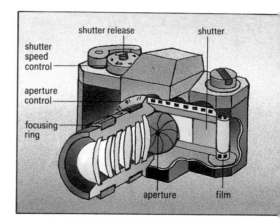

Figure 4
A modern camera.

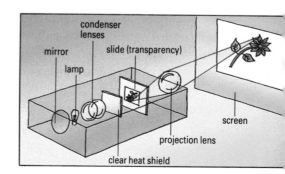

Figure 5
A slide-projector. The curved mirror and the condenser lenses concentrate light from the lamp onto the transparent slide. Then the projection lens casts an image onto the screen.

109

G6 The eye and seeing

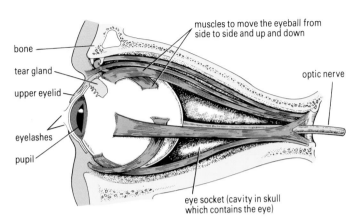

Figure 1
The structure of the eyeball.

bone

tear gland

upper eyelid

eyelashes

pupil

muscles to move the eyeball from side to side and up and down

optic nerve

eye socket (cavity in skull which contains the eye)

ciliary muscle

iris

lens

pupil

cornea

transparent liquid

ligaments

retina

transparent jelly

blind spot

blood vessels

optic nerve (to brain)

Figure 2
Inside the eye.

We use our eyes to see. But how do our eyes work? It is not very difficult to find out. The eyes of animals such as cows, sheep or pigs are very similar to our own. If you have the chance to examine one of these, you will find structures very similar to those shown in figures 1 and 2.

The eye is a bit like a camera – it has a **lens**, and there is a **retina** at the back on which the image falls (see figure 3). Light enters the eye through a hole called the **pupil**. The size of the pupil varies with the intensity of the light (see figure 4).

How does a camera make a sharp image on the film for objects at various distances? If you look at Unit G5, you will see that it does this by changing the distance between the film and the lens. The eye uses a different method of making sharp images of objects at different distances. Its ability to do this is called **accommodation**. Muscles in the eye (called **ciliary muscles**) can cause the lens to change shape, making it fatter or thinner. For distant objects the lens is thin; for close objects the lens is made fatter so that it has greater light-bending power. This ensures that a sharp image is still formed on the retina at the back of the eye. There are limits on how fat the lens can become, so there are limits on how close to the eye an object can be placed and still give a sharp image on the retina. For adults with normal sight, the distance (called the **near point**) is about 20 cm, but you can probably see things closer than that.

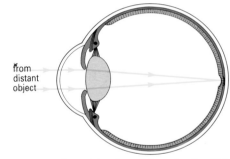

from distant object

focused sharp image is formed on the retina

Figure 3
Forming an image in the eye. Most of the light-bending is done by the cornea.

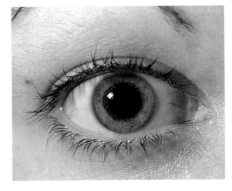

Figure 4
The pupil of the eye in dim light.

Brain 'magic'
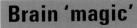

The image on the retina is transmitted to the brain along the **optic nerve**. The brain has to 'make sense' of the nerve impulses it receives. You may already have found out that the image formed by a lens is the opposite way up from the object itself. This means that the picture of the outside world that falls on your retina is upside down! This does not fit in with your brain's other experiences, so it processes the image so that you 'see' the world around you the right way up.

The brain always tries to make sense of the world. It makes the picture we think we see fit in with all its other experiences, past and present. That is why we have to be very careful when we say that 'seeing is believing'. It is often more likely to be 'what we expect to see'!

Getting a clear picture

Even our brains cannot deal with fuzzy pictures! Many people have eyeballs that are slightly distorted. If the eyeball is longer from front to back than it should be, then the sharp image of a distant object will be formed in front of the retina and only close objects will be seen sharply. People whose eyes are like this are said to be **short-sighted**. Spectacle lenses can restore their vision to normal. They need a lens that 'unbends' the light a bit, so that the image of a distant object falls on the retina when the ciliary muscles are relaxed (see figure 5).

A less common defect is **long sight**. Here the eyeball is slightly shorter, from front to back, than it should be. People whose eyes are like this can see distant objects clearly, but their near point is further from the eye than normal and they have difficulty in reading comfortably. Again, spectacles can be used. This time the spectacle lens has to bend the light some more, so making it possible to see close objects clearly (see figure 6).

People also find it increasingly difficult to see things close to their eyes as they get older, because the eye loses some of its power of accommodation. The near point gets further from the eye, and it becomes difficult to read in comfort. Spectacle lenses that produce additional light-bending will help the eye lens for close work.

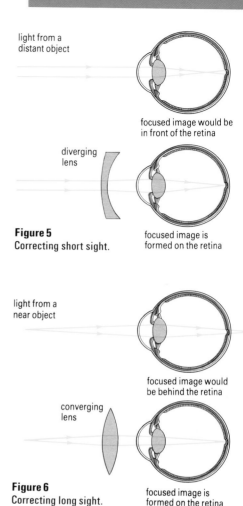

Figure 5
Correcting short sight.

light from a distant object

focused image would be in front of the retina

diverging lens

focused image is formed on the retina

Figure 6
Correcting long sight.

light from a near object

focused image would be behind the retina

converging lens

focused image is formed on the retina

Another common sight defect is **astigmatism**. Find out what this is.

Figure 7
More and more people are now wearing contact lenses instead of spectacles. Contact lenses may be hard or soft. Both sorts are placed on the cornea itself. The natural eye liquids hold the lens in place. Such lenses need care in fitting and use.

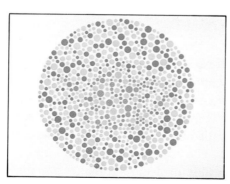

Figure 8
Some people have difficulty in distinguishing between red and green colours. Coloured patterns made up of dots, like the one above, are used to test for this condition.

Figure 1

Magnifying glasses

Hold your arm out at full stretch and look at the end of your finger. How much detail can you see? Now bring your hand closer. Do you notice that you can see more detail? When we want to examine an object, we get closer to it so that we may see it more clearly. But if we get very close we find that we cannot focus on the object, no matter how good our eyes are. This is when we need a magnifying glass.

A magnifying glass helps our eyes to focus on very close objects. This means that we can see the objects much more clearly. If we have normal vision, we may feel uncomfortable if we look at an object that is closer than about 20 cm. With a $10 \times$ magnifying glass, we can bring the object up until it is only 2 cm away, yet still see it clearly. This means that the object seems to be ten times larger. We say that the **magnification** is '$10 \times$'.

Figure 2
Using a magnifying glass helps us to focus on very close objects.

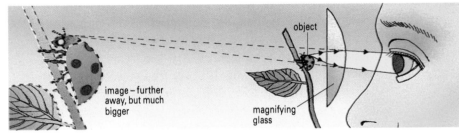

Figure 3
How an image is formed in a microscope.

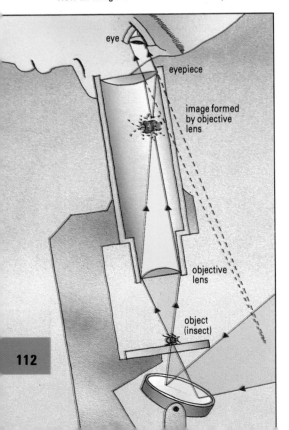

Microscopes

If we want to see very small things, such as cells (see Unit F1), we may want a magnification of several hundred times. To get such a high magnification, we have to use two lenses together.

Figure 3 shows a diagram of a microscope. The lens nearest the object is called the **objective** lens. The lens nearest the eye is called the **eyepiece**.

The objective lens in a microscope is used in the same way as the lens in a slide-projector. It makes a magnified image of the object and places it close to the eyepiece. The eyepiece is a magnifying glass. It helps the eye to get close to the image in the microscope tube and yet still see it clearly.

If the objective lens produces an image that is 20 times bigger than the object and the eyepiece has a magnification of $10 \times$, then the magnification of the whole microscope will be 20×10, that is 200 times.

Telescopes

We can make a telescope in the same way as we make a microscope. Figure 4 shows an arrangement that was first used by Galileo Galilei in 1609. The objective lens forms an image of the object close to the eyepiece. Then the eyepiece lets the eye get close to the image to see it clearly.

Figure 4
How an image is formed in a telescope.

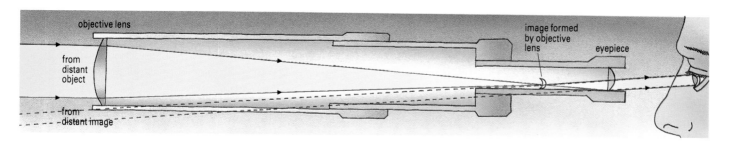

Although the telescope works in the same way as the microscope, there is a problem with it that we do not worry about with microscopes. Both the microscope and the telescope produce images that are upside down. This doesn't usually matter with microscopes. If it does, we can usually turn the *object* upside down. But it is very difficult to look at objects on Earth if their images are upside down!

On the other hand, if we are looking at objects in space, like the Moon, the other planets and the stars, it doesn't really matter which way up the image is. So this simple sort of telescope is often used for looking at astronomical objects. That is why it is called an **astronomical telescope**.

1 Some of the most powerful astronomical telescopes use a mirror for the objective, rather than a lens. See if you can find out why this is.

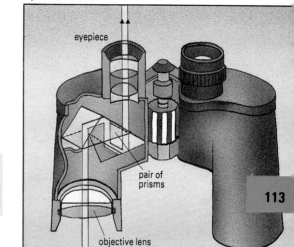

Figure 5
A large refracting telescope in an observatory.

Figure 6
A pair of binoculars.

Binoculars

The astronomical telescope could be used for looking at objects on Earth if the image could be turned the right way up. This is done in binoculars by means of a pair of glass blocks called **prisms** (see figure 6). The glass blocks make up two corner reflectors (see Unit G4). The reflections that take place at these prisms turn the image the right way up. The reflectors have the added bonus of shortening the 'telescope tube' to make binoculars a reasonable size.

2 Apart from turning the image the right way up, what other advantages do binoculars have over the simple telescope?

eyepiece

pair of prisms

objective lens

113

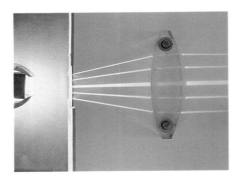

Figure 1
What causes a lens to bend rays of light?

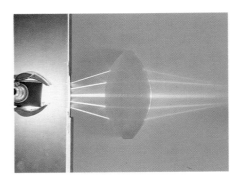

Figure 2
Why do fat lenses bend light more than thin lenses?

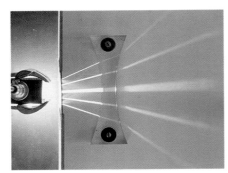

Figure 3
Why do some lenses converge light and some lenses diverge it?

Figure 4
Light being bent by a glass block.

Figure 5
A light ray passing through a prism.

If we want to know why lenses behave as they do (see figures 1, 2 and 3), we first need to look at simpler-shaped blocks of glass.

Figure 4 shows an experiment you may have done with a ray streak of light passing through a glass block. Can you see what happens? The ray streak changes direction as it enters the glass block and again as it leaves it. This bending of light when it goes from one transparent substance to another is called **refraction**.

The ray of light shown in figure 4 finally travels in the same direction as it was taking before it entered the block. If we want to *change* the direction of a ray of light, we need a differently shaped piece of glass. In figure 5, light is being sent through a triangular glass block called a **prism**.

The light ray changes direction as it enters the prism and again as it leaves it. But this time it no longer travels in the same direction after leaving the prism as it did before entering it.

If the ray of light entering the prism is white, the light emerging from the prism can be seen to be broken up into colours.

The study of colour is a very interesting and important area of science. You may be given details of some investigations you can do, either now or later on in science.

Figure 6 shows a group of differently shaped pieces of glass. Can you see what they do to five rays of light that are spreading out? The rays are spreading apart at first. But after they have passed through the glass blocks they are coming together. The glass blocks work in just the same way as a converging lens.

A diverging lens is thin in the middle and fat on the outside. Figure 3 shows how this spreads out a series of rays. The rays falling on the lens are already spreading out. But after passing through the lens, they are spreading apart even more.

Figures 1 and 2 show rays passing through converging lenses. Which way do the rays bend as they pass from air to glass and from glass to air? Do the rays bend the same way as they do when travelling through prisms?

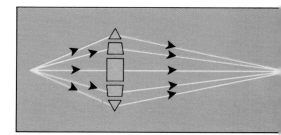

Figure 6
A lens can be thought of as a series of prisms.

Optical illusions

We see refraction happening in other transparent materials as well. If we look at a fish in a fishpond, it appears to be closer to the surface than it really is.

Figure 7 shows how rays of light from the fish get into our eyes. The rays bend as they go from the water to the air. When they reach our eyes, they are travelling in a different direction from their original direction. We are tricked by the rays our eyes receive. We think that the fish is above its actual position. Do you remember another situation in which our eyes can be tricked in the same way? Look back at Unit G4 to remind yourself.

The bending of light when it goes from water to the air causes another optical illusion. When a pencil is partly under water, it appears to be bent. Figure 8 shows what happens to the rays from the pencil as they pass from the water to the air.

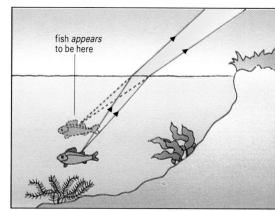

Figure 7
Refraction makes the fish look closer to the surface than it really is.

Mirages

Have you ever been cycling or driving along a road on a hot summer's day and noticed that there seem to be pools of water on the road, even though it hasn't been raining? This effect is called a **mirage**. It is produced by light from the sky bending in the hot air near the road. Your brain thinks the rays of light entering your eye come from the road itself. The patch of sky that you see looks just like reflections in a pool of water.

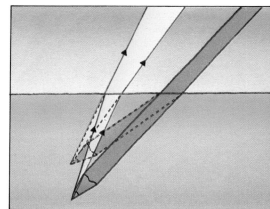

Figure 8
The refraction of light as it passes from the water to the air makes the pencil look bent.

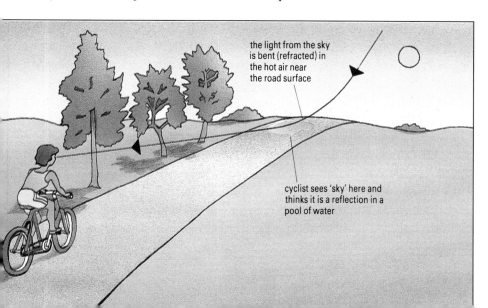

the light from the sky is bent (refracted) in the hot air near the road surface

cyclist sees 'sky' here and thinks it is a reflection in a pool of water

Figure 9
How mirages are formed.

115

Have you ever looked at the sky on a clear night and wondered what is out there? People have done this for thousands of years, asking questions such as 'What are stars?', 'What are they made of?' and 'Why do they form fixed patterns in the sky?' **Astronomers** are people who try to answer this sort of question. But first they need to collect more information. How do they do this?

Observing

It is difficult to learn much about the Universe just by using your eyes. But if you look at the sky night after night, you soon realize that the patterns of stars (called **constellations**) seem to rotate in the sky. Figure 1 shows a photograph of the sky at night. The shutter of the camera was kept open for an hour or so. The streaks were made by images of the stars while the photograph was being taken. The stars seem to rotate about a point in the sky. That point is directly above the Earth's North Pole.

To find out more about the stars by looking at them, you really need to use a telescope. Much of the light that arrives on the Earth from the stars is very faint. With big telescopes, more of this light can be collected. This is usually done by using big mirrors. The reflecting telescope shown in figure 2 has a mirror five metres in diameter. If a camera is used to make time-exposures of the star images, even more information can be collected from the faint light arriving on Earth.

The star light can be split up into its colours by passing the light through a prism. Astronomers can learn a great deal about the insides of stars from the colour of their light. Radio waves from stars can also be picked up on the Earth's surface. These radio waves are detected by radio telescopes, such as the one shown in figure 3. Radio telescopes work in a similar way to the reflecting telescope shown in figure 2.

Observations show that the Sun is just one star in the Universe. Light from the Sun and the stars shows us that there are other objects that do not shine by their own light. Some of these objects are clearly visible in the night sky. They seem to move about against the star background, and hundreds of years ago they were given the name **planets**, which comes from the Greek word for 'wanderer'.

One problem with making observations from the Earth is its atmosphere. This gets in the way of the light and can make observation very difficult. In recent years, telescopes have been placed on satellites orbiting the Earth and observations can be made from far above the atmosphere.

Figure 1
This is a time-exposure of the night sky. Until a few hundred years ago, people thought that these star trails were produced by the stars rotating around the Earth. Nowadays we say that they are due to the Earth spinning on its own axis. Try to find out more about why we prefer this explanation.

Figure 2
A reflecting telescope at the Mount Palomar Observatory, USA.

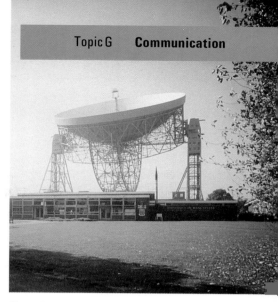

Figure 3
The world's first steerable radio telescope, at Jodrell Bank, Cheshire, UK.

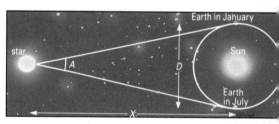

Figure 4
By knowing the diameter of the Earth's orbit around the Sun, and the angle *A*, astronomers can calculate the distance to the star. In practice, the angle *A* is very, very small – a tiny fraction of one degree.

Figure 5
The Andromeda galaxy. Astronomers have shown that this galaxy is 2 200 000 light-years from the Earth.

Probing

Observing is rather like being a 'bird-watcher' of the Universe – we set up our telescopes and wait patiently for something to happen. But instead of relying on signals (light or radio waves) that objects such as planets happen to send to us, *we* could send signals to *them*. You can read about an example of this in Unit G4, where there is a description of laser light being bounced off a reflector on the Moon.

Sending out a signal and detecting its return is called **probing**. This is much more like carrying out an experiment on Earth. So far, probing has only been used to find out things about our near neighbours. For example, radio waves have been bounced off the planet Venus and used to measure its distance from the Earth with great accuracy. Venus and the Earth are two planets among nine, orbiting the Sun. This group of the planets and the Sun is referred to as the **Solar System**. It is approximately 12 000 million kilometres in diameter.

Measuring distances in the Universe

Figure 4 shows how astronomers can find the distance from the Earth to the nearer stars. They do it by finding the direction of the light from a star at different times of the year, when the Earth is at opposite points of its orbit around the Sun. Such measurements have shown us that even the nearest stars (other than the Sun) are much further away than the planets. In fact, even the nearest star is so far away that its distance is measured in light-years. One light-year is the distance a pulse of light travels in one year. The nearest star is 4.3 light-years away, and the average distance between stars is about five light-years. By comparison, it would only take a light pulse about eleven hours to cross the entire Solar System.

To measure even larger distances, astronomers can rely on the fact that an object like a star will appear to be fainter and fainter the further away it is from the Earth. Astronomers know how bright one particular type of star (called a 'Cepheid variable') should be at any given distance from the Earth. By picking out these stars and measuring their brightnesses, astronomers can work out how far away they are. From these and other measurements, astronomers have discovered that all the individual stars you can see with the naked eye are clustered together in a galaxy which is almost 200 000 light-years in diameter. Beyond this there are other galaxies, such as the one shown in figure 5 which is our own galaxy's near neighbour – a mere 2 200 000 light-years away!

Why do you think probing is unlikely to be useful for investigating stars?

G10 Visiting the planets

Figure 1
The *Voyager* spacecraft travelled outwards on spiralling paths, using the gravitational pull of the planets to help them on their way.

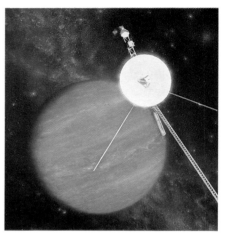

Figure 2
Voyager 2 approaching Neptune. Why does it not need to have a streamlined shape?

Figure 3
Some planets and moons, like Io, shown in this picture, have active volcanoes.

Figure 4
Jupiter's red spot is a stable cloud pattern three times bigger than the Earth itself.

Even the biggest telescopes on Earth give us very little information about the planets. To find out more, scientists have used spacecraft.

The planets are very far apart and journeys to them can take many years. In 1978 the United States launched two spacecraft, called *Voyager 1* and *Voyager 2*, to explore the outer planets. The spacecraft travelled outwards on spiralling paths, using the gravitational pull of the planets to help them change direction as they journeyed from one planet to the next (see figure 1). *Voyager 2* travelled outwards at a speed of more than ten kilometres per second. Even so, it took twelve years to reach Neptune, the last planet on its journey. Such long trips are not yet possible for astronauts, so scientists control these **space probes** (as these unmanned spacecraft are called) from Earth.

A typical space probe is shown in figure 2. The large dish sends radio signals back to Earth and also receives commands for the probe's computer. Space probes travelling inwards towards the Sun are powered by solar panels which convert sunlight to electricity. Probes to the outer planets carry a small nuclear generator to provide their power.

Most space probes carry a television camera which sends pictures of the planets and their moons back to Earth. Telescopic lenses are fitted to take close-up pictures so that geologists can study landscapes of the solid planets and moons. For example, they have discovered that one of Jupiter's moons, called Io, is covered by active sulphur volcanoes.

A television camera is not always useful, though. The surface of Venus is permanently hidden by a thick cloudy atmosphere, so its landscape has been mapped from orbiting space probes by using radar instead. The Earth's ocean floors have been mapped in the same way.

Most space probes carry a **magnetometer**, which measures the planet's magnetic field. This can tell us if the planet has a core of a magnetic substance such as iron or nickel (see Unit I2).

Another useful instrument is a **spectrometer**, which splits light into its separate colours like a prism (see Unit G8). The light reflected off planetary atmospheres can tell us about the gases that they contain.

Data from the space probes has also enabled scientists to measure the gravitational pull of the planets and their moons. From these and other measurements, they can work out the average density of a planet or a moon, and this gives a clue about what it is made of. For example, the planet Mercury is rather dense, which suggests that it has a large metallic core like the Earth. The moons of the outer planets have low densities and are probably mainly composed of ice.

So far, spacecraft landings have only been made on our own moon, and on Mars and Venus. American space probes successfully landed on Mars in the mid-1970s. Using remote control, scientists tested soil samples for signs of life, but did not find any. They also found that the atmosphere was mainly carbon dioxide and very thin, while the surface was a very cold desert. They came to the conclusion that it is unlikely that there is life on Mars at present.

Early Soviet space probes to Venus stopped working as they descended to its surface. It was soon discovered that its atmospheric pressure at ground level is 90 times that of the Earth, and that the temperature is over 450 °C! The later probes were much stronger and managed to survive a few hours. They were able to send back pictures of Venus' surface.

What of the future? The United States intends to send more space probes to Jupiter and Saturn, and the Soviet Union is planning a two-year manned trip to Mars.

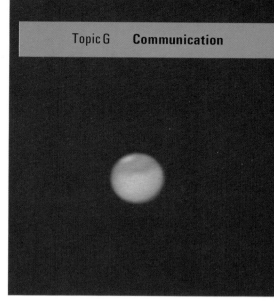

Figure 5
Astronomers can find out little about Mars from photographs taken from the Earth.

Figure 6
This photograph was taken from 560 000 km above the planet's surface and shows much more detail.

Figure 7
This picture was taken by the *Viking* space probe, which landed on the surface of Mars.

119

WHY WE BELIEVE THE EARTH IS ROUND!

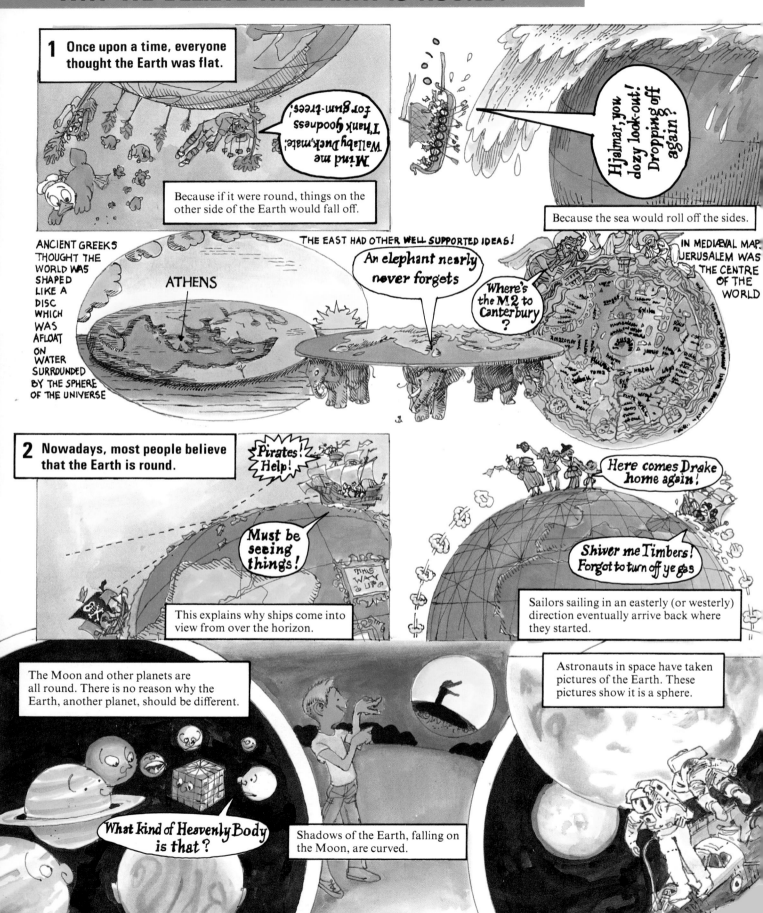

Topic **H Rocks, minerals and metals**

H1 The Earth's crust

Centuries ago, people thought that many rocks were produced by a great fire in the centre of the Earth – they knew that volcanoes poured molten rock onto its surface. We still use the word **igneous** (which means 'fire-produced') for rocks that were once molten, but we now believe that they come from a very hot layer some way beneath the Earth's surface.

The Earth is a sphere almost 13 000 km in diameter. It is covered by a thin **crust** of solid rock, between 5 km and 40 km thick, which surrounds it like a shell (see figure 1). Below this, scientists believe that there is a layer of partly molten rock called the **mantle**. The crust is made of a dark dense rock called basalt and is divided into plates that float on the mantle beneath. Molten basalt is continually flowing up through some of the joins between the plates, pushing them apart. This process pushes one plate against another somewhere else. One plate goes underneath – back to the hot mantle – and the other rides over the top.

What evidence is there for this model of the Earth's crust? Figure 2 is a map of the Earth's surface showing where most volcanic and earthquake activity occurs. Lines can be drawn through these regions of intense Earth activity. Scientists think that these lines mark the edges of the plates.

There is intense volcanic activity going on along the centre of the Atlantic Ocean. This is a line of **upwelling** rock. As the upwelling occurs, a mountain ridge is built which sometimes projects above the surface of the sea. This upwelling causes the plates to move apart a few centimetres every year. Other lines of upwelling rock run through the Indian and Pacific Oceans. Lines of upwelling rock are almost always found on ocean beds, so this process is called **ocean-floor spreading** (see figure 3).

Along the western edge of the Pacific Ocean there is a different sort of plate margin. Here, deep ocean trenches, earthquakes and a curved line of

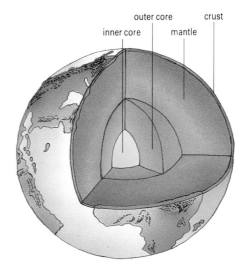

Figure 1
The structure of the Earth.

Figure 2
The lines of volcanic and earthquake activity mark the edges of the plates.

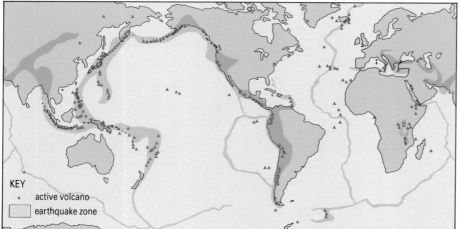

KEY
▲ active volcano
☐ earthquake zone

122

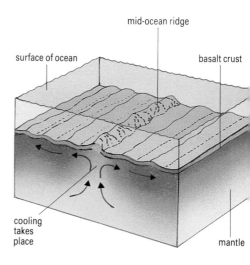

Figure 3
Ocean-floor spreading.

islands rising up from the ocean all suggest that one plate is moving downwards beneath another.

Embedded in the moving plates are huge slabs of a lighter coloured, less dense igneous rock called granite. These slabs form the bases of the Earth's land masses and are known as the **continental shields**.

The rocks of the continental shields are constantly being attacked by rain, wind, ice and rivers. The rocky particles are carried off by rivers to be deposited in horizontal layers around the edges of the continents. The weight of this eroded material presses the particles together to form new rocks, called **sedimentary** rocks.

When a plate with a continental shield at its edge is pushed against another plate, the edge of the continental shield buckles up in long mountain chains, folding and faulting any layers of sedimentary rocks there (see figure 4). This is happening in several parts of the world. Once these new mountain chains are formed, the process of erosion starts all over again (see figure 5).

Plate activity produces regions of intense heat and pressure. These can affect sedimentary and igneous rocks in the neighbourhood, producing yet another type of rock. Limestone (a sedimentary rock) can be changed into marble, for example, and granite (an igneous rock) into gneiss. Rocks changed in this way are called **metamorphic** rocks.

So the continental shields are made partly of igneous rocks, and partly of sedimentary and metamorphic rocks. Most of the minerals and ores used in industry are taken from the sedimentary rocks – for example, iron, aluminium and magnesium. Other important metals, especially copper, lead and zinc, are found in igneous rocks. Petroleum and coal, which are the products of the decay of animals and plants, are found in sedimentary rocks.

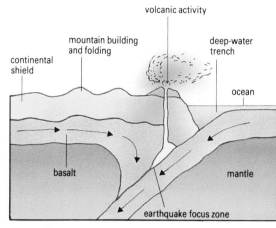

Figure 4
Mountain building at a plate margin.

Figure 6
Examples of igneous, sedimentary and metamorphic rocks.

a Basalt (igneous).

b Sandstone (sedimentary).

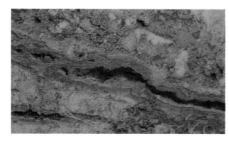

c Marble (metamorphic).

Figure 5
Rocks are continually being eroded and rebuilt.

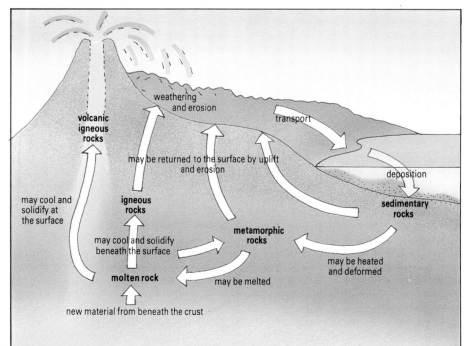

123

H2 Using rocks and minerals

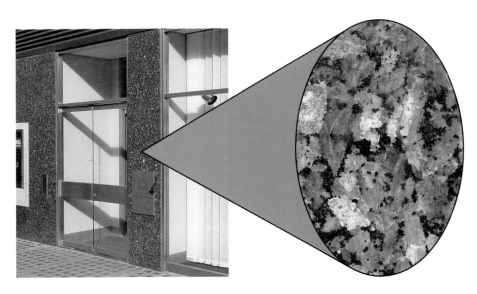

Walking along a street, you can sometimes see a fine collection of rocks that have been used to decorate the fronts of shops, banks and offices. One of the most popular is larvikite, an igneous rock which sparkles with enormous crystals of feldspar. The black mineral in the rock is magnetite. This rock is only found in southern Norway, near the small town of Larvik.

Another popular building material is Portland stone. This is a limestone from a peninsula on the coast of Dorset. It is a sedimentary rock that was formed under the sea 140 million years ago.

Some grand buildings are decorated with rare minerals. This room in the Winter Palace in Leningrad is magnificently ornamented with green malachite.

Marble is a metamorphic rock that is formed when limestone is re-crystallized by heating and pressure.

Graphite is a black mineral which is valuable because it is so soft. Mixed with clay it is used to make pencil 'leads'. Soft 'B' pencils have more graphite and less clay than harder 'H' pencils. Graphite can also be used instead of oil, as a lubricant. Chemically, graphite is an element: it is pure carbon.

Elijah McCoy was the son of Kentucky slaves who escaped to Canada, where he was born. He trained as a mechanical engineer in Scotland. He could not get a job as an engineer when he returned to the United States, so he worked as a fireman on the railways. In those days, steam engines had to stop from time to time to be lubricated with oil. McCoy invented an 'automatic lubricator' and patented it in 1872. This lubricator was soon used all over the world and train crews would check to make sure that their locomotive was fitted with 'the real McCoy'. In 1915 he developed a lubricator which used powdered, solid graphite instead of oil.

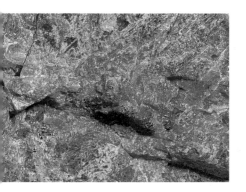

Some minerals are valuable as abrasives because they are very hard. One example is corundum, which is the next hardest mineral after diamond. It is a compound of aluminium and oxygen. Emery is a greyish-black form of corundum that is used to make abrasive papers.

Bricks which line furnaces may have to stand temperatures up to 2000 °C. Minerals which will not melt at these high temperatures are called **refractories**. This furnace is lined with bricks made of magnesite.

Metals come from minerals in rocks. This is a sample of chalcopyrite – a copper ore.

Draw up a table to show how the uses of minerals and rocks are related to their properties. Start with the examples on these pages but then add others which you know about from your own experience. Use these headings:

Name of the rock or mineral	Uses	Properties which make it useful

125

H3 Jewellery

Since early times, people have used materials to produce beautiful body adornments. Here you can see some of the wonderful things that have been fashioned from metals, gem-stones, glass, ceramics and plastics.

Gold has been used for jewellery since ancient times. Here you can see it in necklaces from Egypt, which are over 3000 years old, and being worn by a guest at a banquet. As gold is very unreactive, it occurs as a metal in nature. It is easy to shape and does not react with the air when melted.

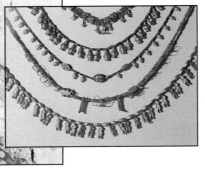

This necklace (or torc) is made from bronze and is about 2000 years old. It would have been worn by the chief of a tribe. Bronze is a mixture of copper and tin that is made from a mixture of metal ores. Metal mixtures such as bronze are called **alloys**.

This brooch is from the 1920s and is made from enamel supported on a copper base. It is designed in the Art Deco style, which was developed in France after the First World War. It would have been worn by fashion-conscious young women. Enamel is a type of glass.

Plastics provide the possibility of inexpensive and attractive jewellery that everyone can afford. You can make a brooch like this by gluing pieces of acrylic plastic together into a block (laminating) and then 'slicing off' and polishing.

Couples often exchange engagement rings when they decide to marry. Those worn by women are usually made of gold and decorated with precious stones such as diamonds, rubies or emeralds. When members of the Royal Family become engaged there is great interest in the ring.

Titanium metal can provide a range of colours without being dyed. Its oxides are brightly coloured, so heating the metal in air with a blow-torch forms layers of coloured oxides. Different colours are produced by making some parts hotter than others.

Inexpensive materials are now used in 'everyday' jewellery that most people can afford. The leather strap supports pieces of aluminium that have been anodized and then dyed. Anodizing is a process which uses electrolysis (see Unit H5) to form a layer of aluminium oxide on the surface of the metal. Aluminium oxide holds onto dyes strongly, so the aluminium can be covered with a coloured coating.

Clay has been used for jewellery since ancient times. The lapel-pin was shaped from clay while it was soft. The clay was then dried and fired to turn it into a hard ceramic. The clay was coloured with a coating of glaze, which is a type of glass. Ceramics and glass are made from cheap raw materials such as clay and sand, but this jewellery is expensive because of the skill and time which went into making it.

127

H4 The chemistry of iron-making

Iron is extracted from **iron ore** in a **blast furnace** (see figure 1). The furnace gets its name from the blast of hot air that is blown in at the bottom.

The chemical reactions in the furnace remove impurities from the ore and take away the oxygen from the iron oxide to leave the metal. The process of removing oxygen from a compound is called **reduction**.

Figure 1
A blast furnace.

Iron is the second most common metal in the Earth's crust after aluminium. The main ore is the mineral **haematite**, which consists of iron oxide, Fe_2O_3. High-grade ore contains up to 60 per cent of iron. The impurities are sand and clay.

Another essential raw material for iron-making is **coke**, which is mainly made up of the element carbon. It is produced by heating coal and has three jobs to do in the furnace:

- It is strong enough to hold up the mixture of iron oxide and limestone, but porous enough to allow gases to rise to the top.

- It burns in the air blast at the bottom to heat the furnace:

  carbon(s) + oxygen(g) $\longrightarrow$ carbon dioxide(g)

- The carbon dioxide made by burning the coke rises up the furnace and reacts with more coke to form carbon monoxide:

  carbon dioxide(g) + carbon(s) $\longrightarrow$ carbon monoxide(g)

It is carbon monoxide that takes the oxygen away from the iron oxide to leave iron on its own:

iron oxide(s) + carbon monoxide(g) $\longrightarrow$ iron(s) + carbon dioxide(g)

iron ore

coke

limestone

As the iron moves down the furnace, it melts and runs down to collect in a pool at the bottom.

The third raw material is **limestone** (calcium carbonate), which stops the furnace from getting choked up with the impurities in the ore, such as sand (silicon dioxide). Sand does not melt in the furnace but it reacts with lime to form a liquid slag (calcium silicate). Limestone splits up into calcium oxide and carbon dioxide in the hot furnace:

calcium carbonate(s) $\longrightarrow$ calcium oxide(s) + carbon dioxide(g)

The calcium oxide combines with impurities to form the slag:

calcium oxide(s) + silicon dioxide(s) $\longrightarrow$ calcium silicate(l)

The slag runs down to the bottom of the furnace and floats on the surface of the molten iron ore.

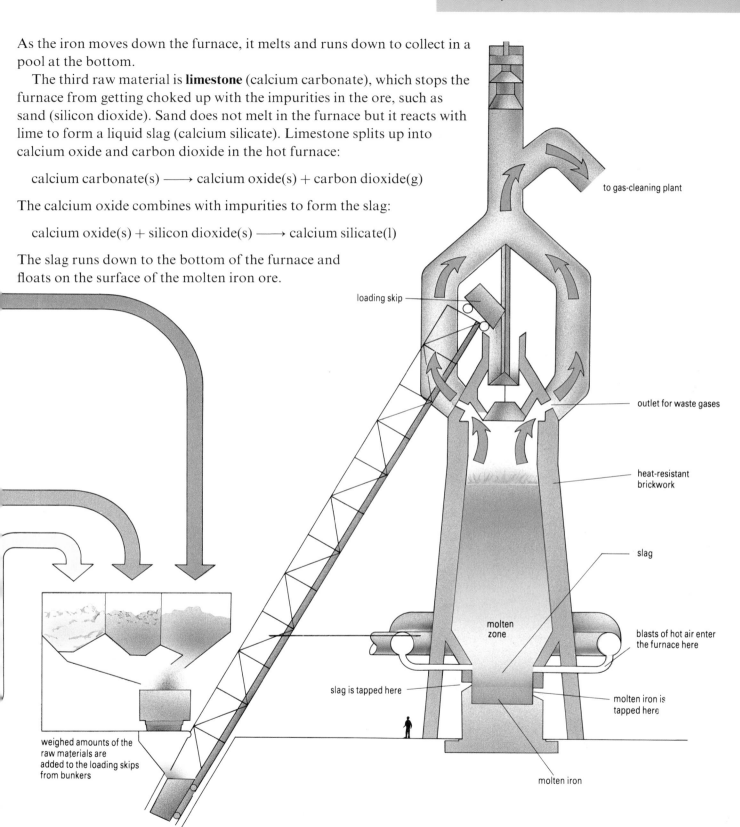

to gas-cleaning plant

loading skip

outlet for waste gases

heat-resistant brickwork

slag

molten zone

blasts of hot air enter the furnace here

slag is tapped here

molten iron is tapped here

weighed amounts of the raw materials are added to the loading skips from bunkers

molten iron

Figure 2
Iron ore, coke and limestone are heated together in the blast furnace to produce molten iron and slag, which are tapped off at the bottom of the furnace from time to time.

H5 Electrolysis

Figure 1

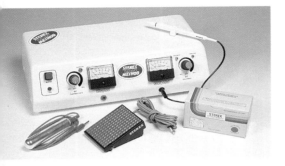

a Equipment used by a firm specializing in hair-removal by electrolysis.

b Using electrolysis to remove hair from the skin.

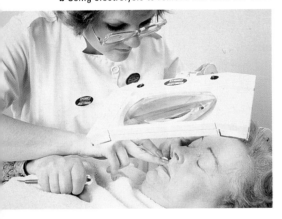

You may have seen electrolysis advertised as a method for removing hair from the skin. What is electrolysis? What does it do?

The word 'electrolysis' is in two parts – 'electro-' for electricity and '-lysis', which comes from the Greek word for 'splitting'. So electrolysis is a method for breaking things into parts using electricity.

Look at figures 2 and 3, which show electric circuits. The bulb lights if a current is flowing. In figure 2, the circuit includes a piece of copper. Copper is a metal, and *all* metals conduct electricity. The copper does not change. However long you pass the electric current, the metal stays just the same.

In figure 3, the circuit includes a tube containing a concentrated solution of copper chloride. The circuit is connected through two black rods, made of graphite, which conduct electricity. The two rods are called **electrodes**.

When the switch is closed the bulb lights, which shows that a current is flowing. So a solution of copper chloride conducts electricity. But something else happens too: there are the changes at the two rods. A gas is bubbling from the electrode attached to the positive terminal of the power-pack, and after a few minutes the other electrode is clearly covered with a pinkish-red coating.

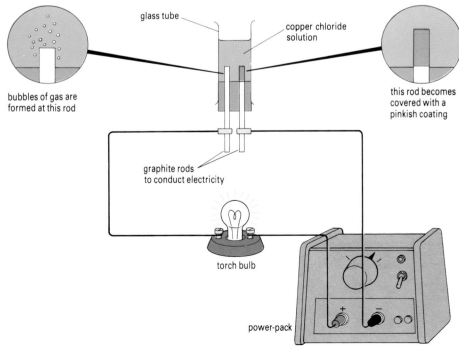

glass tube

copper chloride solution

bubbles of gas are formed at this rod

this rod becomes covered with a pinkish coating

graphite rods to conduct electricity

torch bulb

power-pack

Figure 2

Figure 3
Electrolysis of copper chloride. Look carefully at the changes happening at the two electrodes.

The gas is chlorine and the pinkish solid is copper. In this way an electric current *splits up* the compound copper chloride into two elements – copper and chlorine.

Making use of electrolysis

Electrolysis is a very powerful method for changing things and splitting them up. It is the only method we have for splitting some compounds into elements. Aluminium, magnesium and sodium are all extracted from their ores by electrolysis.

Electrolysis can be used to protect and decorate metals too. A special type of electrolysis called **anodizing** builds a protective coat on aluminium, which can then be dyed (see Unit H3). Steel can be coated with other metals, such as chromium or silver (see figure 4), to give it a bright and shiny appearance.

Figure 5 shows how all materials can be sorted into conductors and non-conductors. The conductors are of two main kinds – metals and electrolytes.

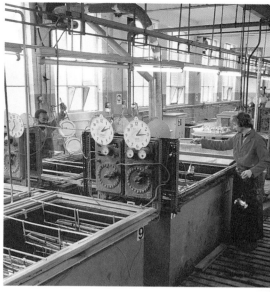

Figure 4
Silver-plating in progress. Here you can see trays being lifted out of the plating solution and tankards being put in.

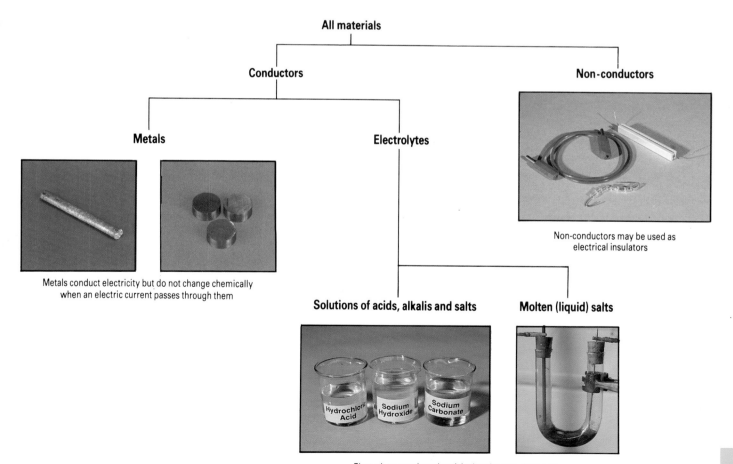

All materials

Conductors

Non-conductors

Metals

Electrolytes

Metals conduct electricity but do not change chemically when an electric current passes through them

Non-conductors may be used as electrical insulators

Solutions of acids, alkalis and salts

Hydrochloric Acid   Sodium Hydroxide   Sodium Carbonate

Molten (liquid) salts

Electrolytes conduct electricity but they are changed by the current which splits compounds into elements

Figure 5

131

H6 Metals and their uses

This guardsman is playing a brightly polished brass instrument. Brass is an alloy of copper and zinc.

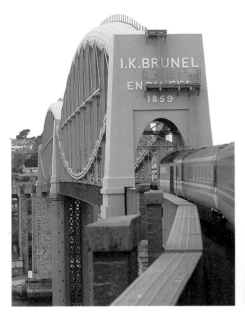

This famous bridge at Saltash carries the main railway line over the river Tamar from Plymouth towards Land's End. The growing iron industry in the nineteenth century produced the metal needed for bridges, rails and locomotives.

Heavy lead bricks are used to build barriers which shield workers from radioactive sources.

Steel is made by purifying and alloying the iron produced in a blast furnace (see Unit H4). The body panels of cars are formed by forcing sheets of steel into shape in powerful presses.

This ornamental boot-scraper comes from New Zealand.
It was made from cast iron in the nineteenth century.

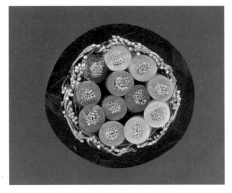

Copper can be drawn out into
wire by forcing it through a die.
Here drawn copper wire is being
coiled up onto large drums.

This cast-iron saucepan is
decorated with enamel.

This cross-section shows the
strands of copper wire in a cable.

The glass bulb of an electric lamp
protects the tungsten filament.
Normally, the filament carries a
higher current and is very hot,
so that it would quickly burn away
in the air.

Most metals are useful because they

- are shiny
- are dense
- bend and stretch
- conduct electricity
- conduct energy from hot to cold
- are often hard and strong
- melt at high temperatures

Find examples of metals being used because they have these properties. Start with
the examples on these pages, but then add others from the metals that you see or
use every day. Make a table of your examples, with these headings:

Name of the metal	Use of the metal	Property which makes the metal useful

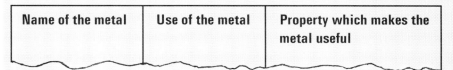

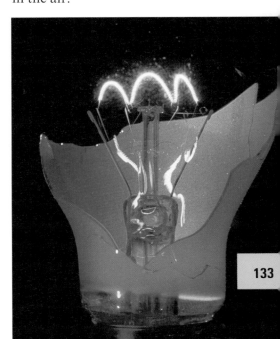

133

H7 The reactivity series of metals

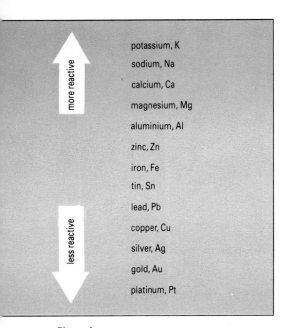

Figure 1
A reactivity series for metals, with the most reactive metal at the top.

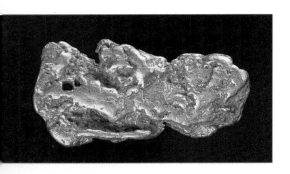

Figure 2
A nugget of gold found free in nature.

What happens if you put a piece of sodium in water? Would the same thing happen with a piece of iron? Because of the differences in the metals' chemical reactivities, it can be useful to draw up a list of them, with the most reactive at the top and the least reactive at the bottom (see figure 1). This **reactivity series** is used to predict what will happen during the chemical reactions of metals.

Metals reacting with the air

Metals at the top of the series react with the air so quickly that they have to be protected from it. Elements such as sodium and potassium are kept in oil to stop them combining with gases in the air (see the pictures in figure 1 on page 54). These metals burn brightly if they are heated in air.

Metals at the bottom of the series are so unreactive that they can be found free in nature. Figure 2 shows a nugget of gold which was found in Australia.

Metals in the middle of the series, such as zinc and iron, react slowly. They combine with oxygen in the air to form **oxides**. This example of **oxidation** is often called **corrosion**. A layer of brown rust forms on iron when it corrodes. Zinc and iron turn to oxides much more quickly when they are heated.

Metals reacting with water and steam

Sodium and potassium, at the top of the reactivity series, react violently with water. Figure 2 on page 54 shows what happens when potassium and water react.

Magnesium is lower in the series, so it reacts very slowly with cold water. This can be demonstrated using the apparatus in figure 3. But it reacts much faster if the water is heated up and turned into steam as shown in figure 4. Only three elements are involved in these reactions –

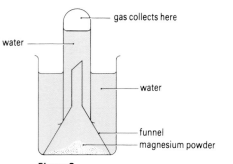

Figure 3
Magnesium reacts very slowly with cold water.

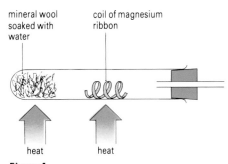

Figure 4
One way of making magnesium react with steam.

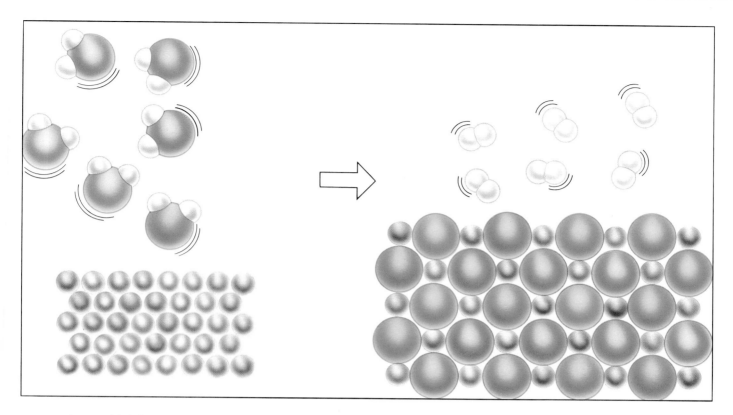

Figure 5
A model equation showing magnesium taking the oxygen from water.

magnesium, which is present as the free element at the start, as well as hydrogen and oxygen, which are joined together in the water.

Magnesium is reactive enough to take away the oxygen from the hydrogen:

magnesium(s) + water (g) $\longrightarrow$ magnesium oxide(s) + hydrogen(g)

The model equation in figure 5 shows this more clearly than the word equation does.

Metals such as copper, which are near the bottom of the reactivity series, do not react with water at all. This makes them useful for water pipes or for covering roofs.

Competition for oxygen

You can think of the reaction of magnesium with water as a competition for oxygen. The hydrogen starts 'in possession' holding onto the oxygen. In the reaction, the magnesium 'wins' and grabs the oxygen from the hydrogen.

Whenever two metals compete for oxygen, the reactivity series can be used to pick the winner. A metal higher in the series holds onto oxygen more strongly than a metal lower in the series. In the thermit reaction (see figure 6), aluminium is used to take away the oxygen from iron oxide.

Zinc can take away the oxygen from lead oxide. The reverse reaction does not go – the zinc keeps hold of its oxygen if you heat a mixture of zinc oxide and lead.

Figure 6
The thermit reaction is used to join sections of railway track together.

135

The world's resources of metals are limited but industrial countries have usually acted as though they can go on exploiting raw materials wherever they are found for as long as they want to.

Using metals brings benefits and problems at every stage, as we mine, extract, process, use and dispose of them. All too often, the gains and losses are not shared fairly between all the people involved. Many metal ores are found in relatively poor countries, but they are exploited economically by richer, more developed countries.

Mineral-processing often involves crushing huge masses of rock to get the small amount of valuable ore. The waste is washed away with water and trapped behind dams.

Mining conditions in some of the poorer parts of the world can expose workers to dust that injures their lungs or to accidents. These tin-miners in Bolivia need the work to feed themselves and their families, but their wages are small.

purifying the ore

mining the ore

Mining conditions can be made safe by careful use of modern technology.

rubbish to waste-tip

A great deal of metal is just thrown away and left to rust on scrap-heaps.

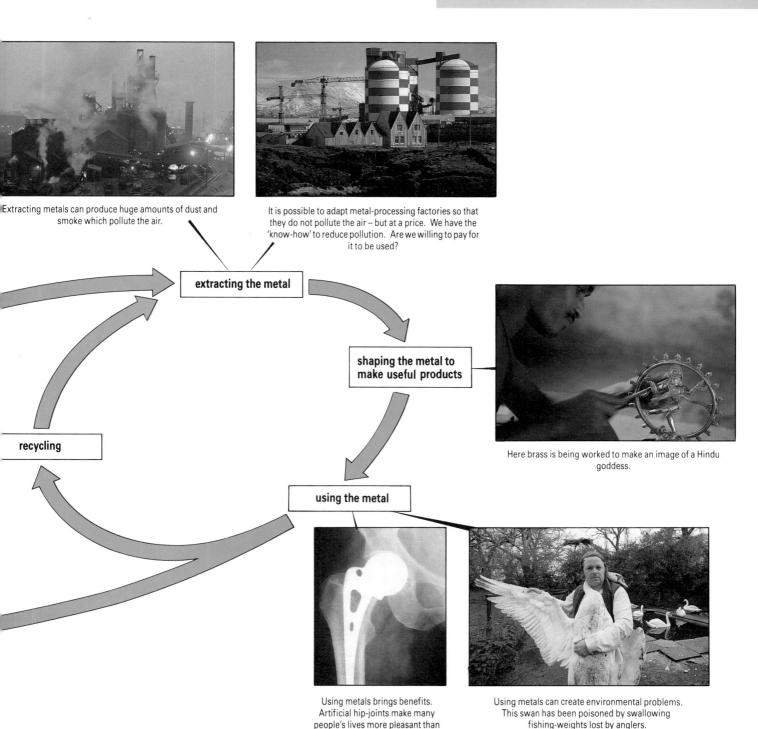

Extracting metals can produce huge amounts of dust and smoke which pollute the air.

It is possible to adapt metal-processing factories so that they do not pollute the air – but at a price. We have the 'know-how' to reduce pollution. Are we willing to pay for it to be used?

extracting the metal

shaping the metal to make useful products

Here brass is being worked to make an image of a Hindu goddess.

recycling

using the metal

Using metals brings benefits. Artificial hip-joints make many people's lives more pleasant than they would otherwise be.

Using metals can create environmental problems. This swan has been poisoned by swallowing fishing-weights lost by anglers.

1 The way we use metals and other mineral resources has benefits and drawbacks. With the help of the information in this unit and in Units H2 and H6, draw up a 'balance sheet' to show some of the gains and losses for people in Britain and for people in other parts of the world. What ways can you think of which might allow more people to share in the gains and fewer people to suffer from the losses?

2 Choose another topic – the use of energy, for example – and see how its benefits and drawbacks compare with those involved in the use of mineral resources.

HOW LONG DOES IT TAKE?

the age of the earth

the plates of the earth shift

mountain ranges rear

hills and valleys form

coasts erode

4.5 BILLION YEARS • 100 MILLIONS • 10 MILLIONS • MILLIONS • CENTURIES • YEARS • MONTHS • DAYS • HOURS • MINUTES • SECONDS

rockfalls

landslide

volcanoes er

sand dunes change

streams change course

Topic I Control

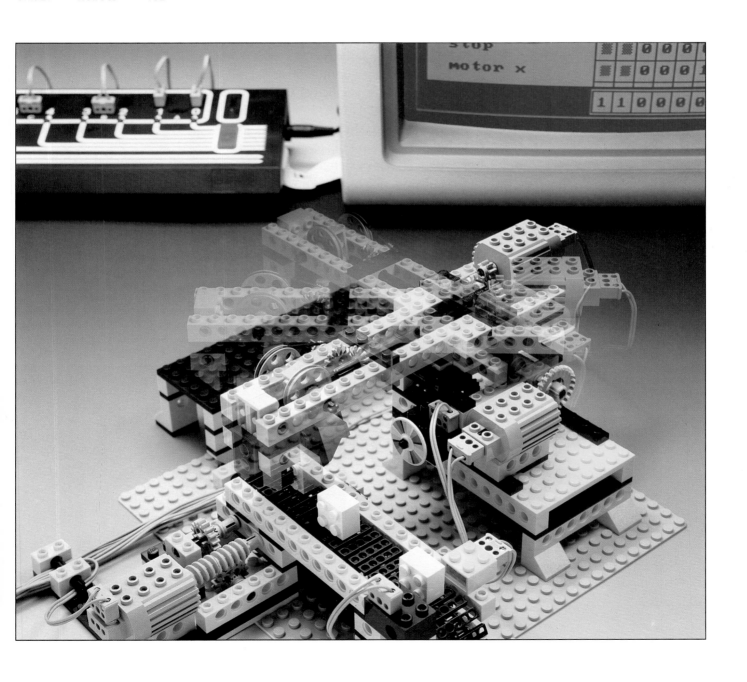

Figure 1
An early locomotive and carriages pictured on a set of postage stamps.

Figure 2
The accident at St John's, Lewisham, in 1957.

This unit is mainly about magnets and magnetism. But it starts by describing a serious problem that magnets have helped to solve – accidents on the railways.

There have been accidents on the railways from the start. William Huskisson MP was killed at the opening of the Liverpool and Manchester Railway in 1830. He was knocked down by the *Rocket*, the locomotive on the set of stamps shown in figure 1. This was a tragic start to one of the first regular steam railways for passengers.

The safety of passengers is of great importance in all transport systems. On railways, drivers need a warning system to tell them whether or not the track ahead is clear. Railways sometimes rely on coloured signal lights to do this. But if the driver does not notice the lights, or if it is too foggy to see them, then an accident could take place. This is what happened at St John's, Lewisham, on 4th December, 1957. On that foggy evening a crowded rush-hour train passed a red signal light. 90 people were killed and 109 seriously injured.

Figure 3
Cabs of present-day locomotives are now equipped with many safety warning devices.

Figure 4
This picture shows the indicator disc that tells the driver whether a warning signal has been acknowledged.

indicator

reset button

Nowadays, an automatic safety system helps avoid accidents such as this. The apparatus used is called the 'Automatic Warning System'. If the way ahead is clear, the signal light by the track shows green. The automatic warning system then rings an electric bell in the driver's cab. Any other colour of signal means that the way ahead is not clear, so the automatic warning system makes a horn sound in the cab. The horn can only be cancelled by the driver pressing a special button. If he does not do this, the brakes go on automatically. Pressing this button also changes an indicator disc in the cab from all-black to a black-and-yellow pattern (see figure 4). This warns the driver that he has cancelled the automatic braking. It is then up to the driver to operate the brakes as needed.

1 Why not do away with the driver and just have a system that automatically puts on the brakes when a signal is red?

2 Why have a number of different warning signals (the signal lights, the bell or horn, and the cab indicator)?

How the automatic warning system works

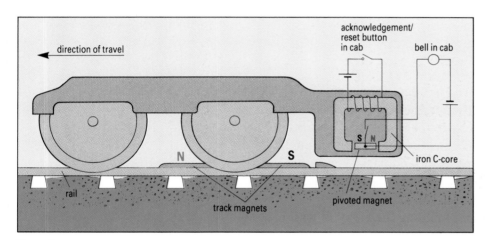

Figure 5
This picture shows the switch under the train that is operated by the track magnets.

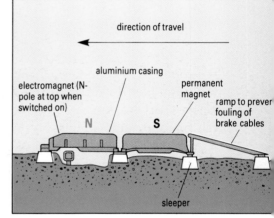

Figure 6
The track magnets that operate the switch under the locomotive.

Figure 7
Track magnets near East Grinstead.

To make the automatic warning system work, there has to be some way of switching it on from outside the train. To do this, there is a switch under the train that can be operated by magnets (see figure 5).

These magnets are fixed between the railway lines, about 200 metres ahead of every signal (see figure 6). This is far enough away for the brakes to be able to stop the train before it passes the signal.

The track magnets come in pairs: one magnet is an electromagnet and the other is a permanent magnet. It is the job of the permanent magnet to close the switch that operates the horn and the automatic braking system. The electromagnet is only turned on when the signal is green. Then the switch under the train rings the 'all clear' bell.

3 Why should it be the permanent magnet that automatically switches on the horn and brakes, rather than the electromagnet?

I2 Finding your way

"Bother! Looks like late detention again!"

Figure 1

Figure 2
Orienteering.

It's good fun to go somewhere new – for a holiday, perhaps, or just a walk. But how do you find your way to somewhere you've never been before? Perhaps you rely on someone else to take you! Explorers often rely on local guides in this way. What if you are on your own, though? You might use a map and rely on signposts or landmarks you can recognize. That is not always possible, though – there are no signposts in the middle of desolate moors, and it is even worse out at sea.

Sailors have always had this problem of finding their way. It was probably more than a thousand years ago that they started using compasses to help them. A compass contains a small pivoted magnet, often referred to as the compass 'needle'. One end of this magnet always points north and the other points south.

The earliest mention of the use of compasses is in a Chinese encyclopaedia written in 1040. Arab traders brought the idea to Europe and the first record of it in Britain is by Alexander Neckham, who was born at St Albans in 1157. He wrote a book, originally in Latin, called *A Treatise on Things Pertaining to Ships* (*All About Ships* in modern English!).

In the reign of Edward III the magnet was known as a 'sail-stone'. The compass was called a sailing needle or dial. The word 'compass' was invented much later. You may have used a compass yourself while orienteering (see figure 2).

What other way is there for sailors to find their direction when out at sea?

Figure 3
A sixteenth-century Italian sailing compass.

Magnetic poles and magnetic fields

If a bar magnet is dipped into iron filings, the filings cluster around the ends, where the magnetic force seems to be concentrated. These regions

142

are called **magnetic poles**. The magnetic pole at the north end of a compass needle is called the north-seeking pole – often shortened to N-pole. The magnetic pole at the other end is called the south-seeking pole or S-pole.

One magnet will attract or repel another magnet. The magnets do not have to touch one another for this to happen. The space around a magnet where its magnetic force can be felt is called the magnet's **magnetic field**. We use the word 'field' in just the same way every day. A field of wheat is somewhere you can find wheat; a magnetic field is somewhere you can find a magnetic force. We sketch magnetic field patterns by drawing lines to show the direction the magnetic force would pull on another magnet's N-pole.

Figure 4
A field of wheat is a place where you will find wheat.

The Earth's magnetic field

A small magnet placed in a magnetic field 'lines itself up' with the direction of the magnetic field. A compass behaves just as though the Earth itself were a giant magnet. The needle lines itself up with the Earth's magnetic field. William Gilbert, one of Queen Elizabeth I's doctors, showed that a sphere made of naturally magnetic iron ore behaved just like the Earth.

You can pivot a compass needle so that it moves up and down rather than from side to side (see figure 6). If a compass needle like this is arranged to point to a magnetized sphere's N-pole, it is seen to dip downwards. The compass needle dips at a steeper angle as it is moved nearer the sphere's magnetic poles. The same thing happens when such a compass needle is put on the Earth's surface. The angle it dips below the horizontal is called the **angle of dip**. Because of this, Gilbert suggested that the Earth was a magnetized sphere. Was he right? Has the Earth got a magnet through its centre? Here are some more facts about the Earth's magnetism that may help you to make up your mind.

A compass needle does not usually point exactly north. In Britain it points about 7° west of north. This angle is called the angle of **magnetic declination.** But that is not all. The magnetic poles keep shifting position and they have even reversed in polarity. Evidence for this has come from rocks in which magnetic material lined up with the direction of magnetic north as it solidified. Reversal of the poles appears to have occurred every 500 000 to 1 000 000 years.

So does the Earth have a large magnet through its centre? Scientists do not think so. Firstly, how could such a magnet keep shifting around? Secondly, at more than a few hundred kilometres below the Earth's surface, the temperatures are too high to allow any material to be magnetic. Above about 1000 °C, iron and similar materials lose their ability to be magnets. Nowadays, scientists think it most likely that the Earth's magnetism is produced by electric currents flowing in part of its molten iron core.

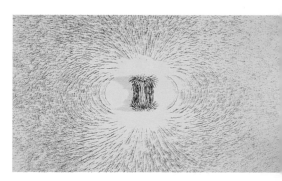

Figure 5
The magnetic field around this magnet is the place where you will find a magnetic force.

Figure 6
A magnet pointing north–south that can move vertically rather than horizontally will point downwards. It is called a **dip circle**.

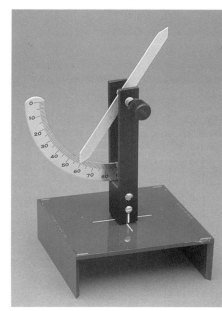

143

I3 Why are magnets magnetic?

Figure 1

'Why are magnets magnetic?' asked Bill.

'What a silly question!' said Jane. 'You might just as well ask why anything is anything! You don't ask why a tree is a tree.'

'I can see Bill and Jane are going to start one of their boring arguments! Let's see if anyone's going to the club tonight,' said Peter.

'No, wait a bit,' said Jane's friend, Anna. 'I think I know what Bill means. You know when Bill was messing around in that last lesson, and he made all those paper-clips into magnets?'

'Yeah,' said Peter, 'an' old Smith nearly threw a fit! He told Bill he could jolly well "unmagnetize" them!'

'Yes,' said Anna, 'but the point is, things which can be magnets aren't *always* magnets. Sometimes they are, but sometimes they aren't.'

'Like the paper-clips,' chimed in Jane.

'Just what I said!' cried Bill. 'Why's a thing that can become a magnet not always a magnet?'

Thinking like a scientist

Asking questions like Bill's is what makes scientists 'tick'. Scientists' questions are often just as difficult to understand, as well. Magnetic materials behave just the way Bill says. They can be made into magnets, but they are not always magnets. So what is a magnetic material like inside that makes it behave this way?

No one can see inside a magnet, so what scientists do is to imagine what it would be like if they *could* see. Making an imaginary picture of things is an important part of doing science. It is called 'making models'. In this unit you will make a model of magnetic materials. This particular model is not a solid thing, like a model ship. It is much more like 'a picture in the mind' – it is 'what you imagine a thing is like'.

Of course, you could imagine anything. But a scientific model has to be more than something you just imagine. It has to be something you can *test*. To understand what this means, we shall invent a model for magnetic materials and then ask you to test it.

Figure 2
Working scientists frequently make models in their heads to try to understand things.

Figure 3
Not all scientific models can be shown as solid objects like this model ship.

A model of magnetic materials

You already have a model for matter in your mind. You have been told it is made up of atoms. Now imagine that magnetic material (iron for example) is made up of lots of particles – they could be atoms, or perhaps clumps of atoms.

Suppose that each one of these particles was itself a magnet. How could you arrange all these particles so that a piece of iron, made up of the particles, was not a magnet itself?

You've probably thought of the answer already. All you have to do is to jumble up the magnetic particles so the little magnets are all pointing in different directions.

What would happen if you stroked this piece of iron with another magnet? If you now do the first experiment in Activity I2, you can see for yourself what might happen.

1 What do you think atoms are like? You can't see atoms. The picture you have in your mind is the 'model'.

Testing the model

If this is a good scientific model, then we should be able to use it to tell us some new things about magnets. This is called 'making predictions'. Here is one question you could ask:

What would happen to a magnet if it was cut in half or heated up?

Think about the model we have invented, then write down your answer. Now try the next experiment in Activity I2. This will test out one of your predictions.

Making explanations

As well as making predictions, models can offer explanations for things we already know about. One thing you know about magnets is that if you heat them up, or knock them about, they lose their magnetism.

2 Use your model of magnetic materials to explain why magnets may lose their magnetism if you knock them about or heat them strongly.

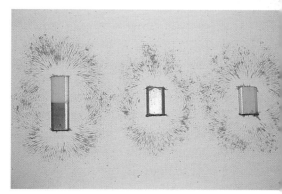

Figure 4
What happens to a magnet if it is cut in half?

Footnote

No matter how well a model seems to work, scientists are always keen to 'see with their own eyes'. Scientists have now been able to grow specially large 'crystals' of iron and to see 'clumps' of magnetism on the surface. The clumps are called **domains**.

When they did this, they discovered that their model was nearly right, but not quite. The magnetic domains certainly point in every direction in unmagnetized iron. But when the iron is magnetized, it isn't that the domains all line themselves up in one direction, but that those pointing the 'right way' get bigger and all the others get smaller.

'So what makes the domains magnetic in the first place?' asked Jane. Well, that's another story (or rather, another model)!

I4 Electricity in use

Figure 1
A busy station in Tokyo, Japan.

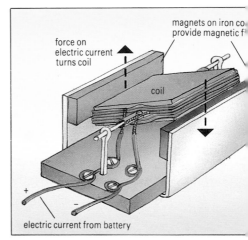

Figure 2
An electric motor that you could build yourself.

The automatic warning system described in Unit I1 uses electricity for control. Electric currents control the electromagnets which are a part of the warning system. But modern railways use electricity for much more than that. How many ways is electricity being used in figure 1?

One thing you have probably said is that electricity is being used to drive the locomotives. (Did you notice the overhead power lines?) Electric currents can make things move by making use of their magnetism. Figure 2 is a diagram of a simple electric motor that you could build for yourself. The electric current flows round the coil of wire, making it into an electromagnet. The permanent magnets at the sides create a magnetic field. This field pulls on the electromagnet and so turns the coil.

Figure 3 is a picture of a pair of electric motors as used in an electric locomotive. You can see that they look a bit different from the simple motor in figure 2, but they work in the same way.

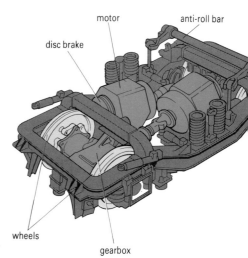

Figure 3
Electric motors in a locomotive.

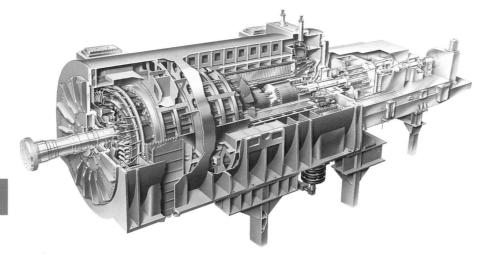

Figure 4
A power-station generator.

Driving an electric current round a circuit

Two things are needed to make a motor work – an electric current and a magnetic field. We can summarize this as:

| ELECTRIC CURRENT | and | MAGNETIC FIELD | gives | MOTION |

Now suppose we write this:

| MOTION | and | MAGNETIC FIELD | gives | ? |

What would you expect to get? You may have guessed that an electric current will flow in the circuit. But of course, as a scientist, you should now test your prediction with an experiment!

This is the way generators in power stations work. You can see a picture of one in figure 4. Making an electric current flow by turning a coil in a magnetic field is called **electromagnetic induction**. It was discovered in the last century by a famous scientist, Michael Faraday (see figure 5).

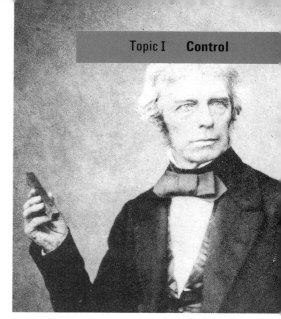

Figure 5
Michael Faraday.

Volts, energy and electricity

You have probably already met and used the word 'volt'. You see it on transistor batteries; you know that the small batteries you use in radios are labelled '$1\frac{1}{2}$ volts', or '$1\frac{1}{2}$ V'. You probably know that the mains electric supply provides 240 volts. The voltage at which electricity is supplied to locomotives is even higher – 25 000 volts. You will also know that such high voltages are very dangerous. But what *is* voltage?

The voltage of an electricity supply tells us something about the energy that can be transferred from one thing to another, using an electric current. The more energy a thing has, the bigger the 'punch' it can deliver – that is why high voltages can be dangerous. So if you wanted a very rough description of voltage, you could think of it as rather like pressure, as something that tells you the force with which currents are driven round the circuit. The important thing to remember, though, is that the voltage of a supply is directly related to the *energy it can transfer*.

You may also know that electric current is measured in units called **amperes** ('amps', or A, for short), using an **ammeter** (see figure 6). The current through the torch bulb in figure 6 is 0.25 A. This is the same as the current through a normally-lit 60 W mains lamp. But in an hour, you would get much more light out of the mains lamp than you would out of the torch bulb. It is the difference in voltage that tells you to expect that.

We measure voltage by using a **voltmeter** (see figure 7). The voltage of the torch battery is 3 V; the mains voltage is 240 V. This means that, in an hour, 80 times as much energy will be transferred from the electricity supply to the mains lamp as from the battery to the torch bulb.

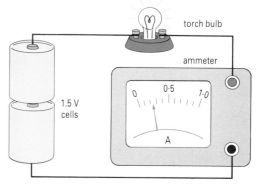

Figure 6
Measuring the current through a torch bulb.

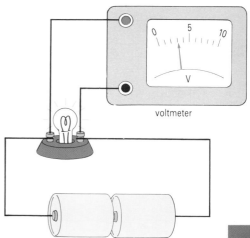

Figure 7
Measuring the voltage across the torch bulb.

147

I5 Electronics

Figure 1

'When I leave school I'm going to get a job in electronics. It's all about computer games, factory robots, hi-fi . . .'

'Well, that sort of thing doesn't interest me at all! I want to do something where I am helping people . . .'

You've all probably talked to one other about your interests and the jobs you want to do when you leave school. Is electronics really about making robots, or could it be about people as well?

Electronics applies the physics of electricity to carrying out useful tasks. Figure 2 shows some everyday objects that depend on electronics.

Hospitals are now able to look after premature babies who are born as much as ten weeks early. These babies need to be watched ('monitored') 24 hours a day. Electronics makes this possible (see figure 3). Developments in electronics also mean that doctors can detect, or 'sense', changes in the human body and display these changes on screens similar to the ones used with computers.

Sensors

'Sensor' is the name we give to any device that can respond to something – for instance light, temperature, sound or pressure – and use it to control an electric current in a circuit. Sensors are often used in electric circuits as a sort of electric switch. You have probably wired up circuits already, in your earlier work in science. Circuits are made up from a number of different parts, called **components**.

Figure 2
This picture shows some devices that use electronics to help them work. Can you think of any others?

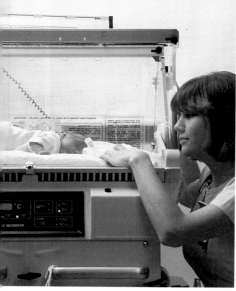

Figure 3
What changes in the human body would doctors and nurses be interested in knowing about, to help them care for a premature baby?

Figure 4
Make a list of all the electric components you can see in this picture.

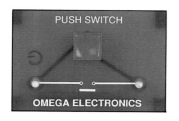

push switch

thermistor

reed switch

light switch

Figure 5
Photographs and circuit symbols of four switches, which respond to different things.

Figure 5 shows pictures of four types of switch that can be used as sensors.

The **push switch** could be described as a sort of pressure sensor, because your fingers provide the pressure needed to close it. Door-bells are often operated in this way.

The **thermistor** is sensitive to changes in temperature. As its temperature changes, so the electric current flowing though it changes. A fire warning device could use one of these.

You may have experimented with magnets already, and you will know that they can magnetize iron. The **reed switch** closes when a magnet is brought near to it.

The **light switch** (usually called a light-dependent resistor, or LDR for short) allows more electricity to flow when light falls on it than when it is in the dark. It can be used to control whether other lights are on or not.

You should be able to try out these sensors for yourself. Because they can only switch on very small electric currents, we have to use a special type of lamp to see them working. These lamps are called **light-emitting diodes** (often shortened to LED).

Figure 6
William Shockley, who helped invent the component called the **transistor**. Without it, modern electronics would be impossible.

149

I6 Control

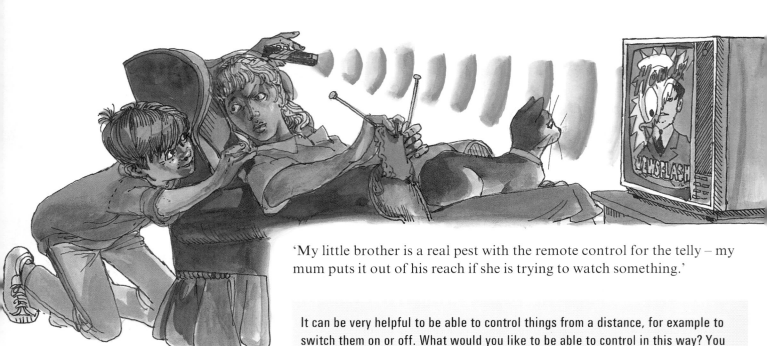

Figure 1

'My little brother is a real pest with the remote control for the telly – my mum puts it out of his reach if she is trying to watch something.'

> It can be very helpful to be able to control things from a distance, for example to switch them on or off. What would you like to be able to control in this way? You might like to illustrate your answer with a cartoon like the one in figure 2.

A television remote control is safe for even very young children to use because electronic devices can use such very small currents (see Unit I5). The television itself also contains electronics, but it uses mains electricity and large currents and voltages. The remote control uses a small current to turn on a much larger one. In all control devices, the control circuit is linked in some way to whatever is being controlled. See if you can find out what links the remote control to the television set.

A **reed relay** is a reed switch which is operated by an electromagnet (see figure 3). It is a useful device for linking a control circuit to something else. Try to learn how to use one by doing some experiments yourself.

Figure 2
A new machine for cleaning out holes in a golf course.

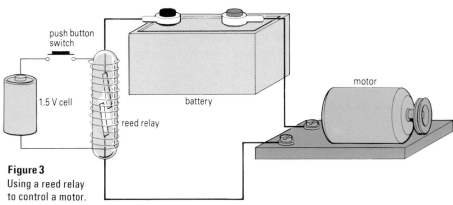

push button switch

1.5 V cell

reed relay

battery

motor

Figure 3
Using a reed relay to control a motor.

Making decisions

We often want electronics to do more than simply switch things on and off for us. It would be very helpful if the control circuits could do some thinking for us as well!

Many people like to have some house lights turned on when it gets dark. If they are at home, they can do it for themselves. Perhaps we could invent a robot to do it for them when they are away from home. To do this job, the robot has to be able to do two things. First of all, it has to be able to turn the lights on and off. Secondly, it has to be able to decide when to do this. The robot has to be able to say to itself, 'There is no light outside, nor is there anyone in the house, so I must switch the lights on.' A statement like that is called a **logical argument**. Some electronic devices, called **logic gates**, can be used to make decisions such as this.

Logic gates

Logic gates are really not much more than electrically-controlled switches. The output 'switch' can be turned on or off by some input 'switches'. A logic gate will either stop a current or allow it to flow through some device connected to its output, depending on how its input switches have been set.

There are a number of different types of logic gate. Each has a word to describe the type of decision it will make and a special symbol to help us draw it. The robot in figure 4 would use a NOR gate. The way it works is shown in figure 5. The robot has to switch the lights *on* if there is neither light outside *nor* anyone in the house. If the 'light outside' information is connected to input A, this will be switched *off* when it is dark. If the 'people in house' information is connected to input B, this will be switched *off* when no one is at home. The house lights, connected to the output of the logic gate, will then be switched *on*.

Figure 4

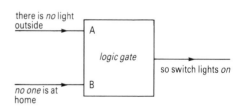

there is *no* light outside → A

logic gate

no one is at home → B

so switch lights *on*

Figure 5
The logic gate used by the robot in figure 4.

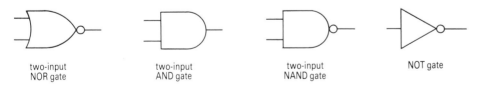

two-input NOR gate

two-input AND gate

two-input NAND gate

NOT gate

Figure 6
Symbols for electronic logic gates.

Figure 6 shows the symbols of four electronic gates. They are called NOR gates, AND gates, NAND gates and NOT gates. 'NAND' is a shortening of the two words 'NOT' and 'AND'.

Once you have learned how to use logic gates, you can invent circuits of your own to do all sorts of jobs. All the devices shown in figure 2 on page 148 use logic gates for control.

I7 Robots

Figure 2 on page 148 shows some of the everyday things that contain electronic control circuits – things like washing machines and sewing machines. At one time, washing machines had to be controlled by hand. The water had to be heated, the time of the wash had to be set, and the washed clothes had to be taken out and put in a spin-drier. Nowadays all of this is controlled automatically by a single 'wash programme'. This sort of automatic control, using electronics, may seem quite complicated, but the decisions the electronic circuits make are really quite simple.

In industry, electronics is used to control much more complicated machines and tools. Machines that make things have to perform a great many complicated tasks, most of which involve movement. Complex machines which can carry out and control difficult movements are usually referred to as **robots**.

Most of us think of robots in the way they are often pictured in science-fiction films – as 'mechanical men' (see figure 1). In fact, they are often designed to do tasks that human beings could do, but which they prefer not to. They may be tasks which are boring or dangerous, or which involve too much effort. Robots never get tired or distracted. They will do a job for the thousandth time with the same accuracy as they did it the first time.

Very few real robots are designed to look anything like humans. Each one is designed to do a particular task – for example, to weld car sections together or to solder up an electronic circuit.

Figure 1
Most people imagine that robots look like these film characters.

Figure 2
This robot is designed to work close to a nuclear reactor – a job it would be too dangerous for a human to do.

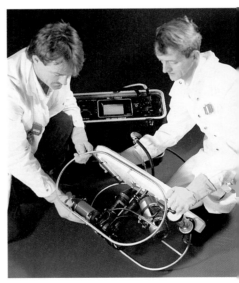

Figure 3
Using robot arms to weld car bodies together.

1 List some of the jobs that you know or believe robots are used for. Could a robot do your science homework for you?

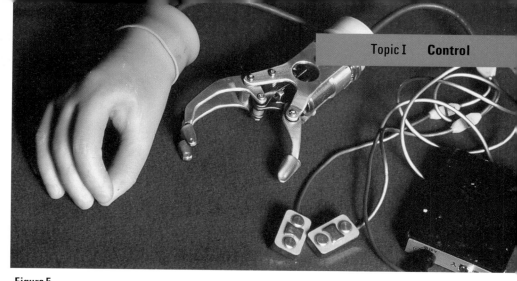

Figure 4
This robot 'guide dog' is able to help blind people.

Figure 5
Artificial limbs involve another sort of automatic control system that works like a robot.

Robots have been developed to work in nuclear power stations. The one in figure 2 works under water and is remotely controlled. The operator, safely away from any nuclear radiation, can control it while watching its actions on a television screen. In car factories a lot of welding and paint spraying is done by robots (see figure 3).

Some robots are designed to help disabled people. The Japanese robot 'Meldog' in figure 4 is an electronic 'guide dog' for the blind. It guides its owner by using a map stored in its computer memory. Ultrasonic sensors, like those used in some automatic focusing cameras, make sure that it 'sees' any obstacles.

Figure 6
Sensors come in all shapes and sizes!

a A sensor to detect moving traffic.

> **2** How does an ultrasonic sensor 'see'? (Think about the underlined letters.)

Robot arms are not only used in industry, but also by people who have lost or damaged their limbs (see figure 5). Some artificial limbs even have a sense of touch.

Many robots need to be able to 'sense' their surroundings, just as we do. Welds on car bodies, for example, have to be made in just the right place. You can read in Unit I5 about sensors that will respond to light, to pressure and to changes in temperature. Electronic sensors can do the jobs of our senses: feeling, seeing, hearing, tasting and smelling. They can be used to feed back information to a robot's control system. Figure 6 shows some of the different types of sensor that you might see around you.

b A sensor to detect smoke.

c Fylingdales 'early-warning' sensors, which would detect missiles.

> **3** Which parts of our body allow us to **a** see, **b** hear, **c** taste, and **d** smell? Try to think of some things an electronic sensor might be able to do that our own sense organs cannot.

The photograph on page 139 shows a model robot that you might be able to build for yourself.

153

Index

(You will, of course, meet more ideas than this in your science work.)

Acknowledgements

Airo: G1.6
Allergan Optical: G6.7
Animal Photography: G3.4
Aspect Picture Library: F5.7
Associated Octel Co. Ltd: A2.1
AVSU King's College: I5.5
Chris Beetles Ltd, St James's, London: I6.2
Biofotos: page 1, B6.4, E5.1, page 77, F4.3a, G3.2, G3.3
Biophoto Associates: F2.2a and b
British Museum: H3.2b
Catherine Blackie: B3.1, C2.1, C4.6, D3.1a, b, and c, D5.2, D5.3, D6.7, D8.8, F1.4, F3.3, F3.6, G2.1 left, G4.1 right, G7.1, page 127 top right, top right (inset), bottom left, and bottom right, page 133 centre left, I3.3
BOC Ltd: A2.3
Boeing: G1.1 bottom right
The Bridgeman Art Library: page 126 right (inset)
Paul Brierley: page 41, H1.6a, b and c
British Coal: page 136 bottom left
British Gas: D5.1
The British Petroleum Company: D5.6
British Rail: I1.3, I1.4, I1.7
British Rail Civil Engineers: H7.6
British Steel Corporation: H4.1, H4.2 top and centre
Camera Press: page 127 top left, I5.6
Central Electricity Generating Board: C3.3
Chris Christodoulou: G1.5
Cloud 9 Photography: I2.2
Bruce Coleman: A1.4, A1.5, page 11, B1.1, B1.3, B1.4, B2.1b, B2.3, B2.4, B3.6, B4.1, B4.2, B4.3, B5.1, B5.2, B5.3, B6.2c, d, e, and f, B6.5, B7.5, B7.6, B7.7, D9.4, page 61, E2.1, E3.4a, F7.3, F10.1a, G1.1 left and top right, G6.4, page 125 bottom left
Colorsport: C2.7
Gene Cox: F3.2, F8.3
Dartington Crystal: A2.6
Geoffrey Dorling: B1.6, B2.6, C2.4
Eastern Counties Newspapers Ltd: B7.3
E.A. Ellison & Co. Ltd: H5.1a and b
Mary Evans Picture Library: C3.5, C4.2, D2.4, G2.5
Fisons/Griffin & George: I2.6
Leif Geiges/Fotografie Werbung: A2.7
GEC Alsthom: I4.4
GEC Transportation Projects: I4.3
Geological Museum: page 121, page 125 bottom right, H7.2
Sir Alexander Gibb & Partners: C6.3
Glass Design and Decoration Ltd: D8.6
Sally & Richard Greenhill: F5.5, F7.5b
Robert Harding: C6.4, page 124 bottom left, page 137 top right, page 137 centre right, I4.1, I7.6c
HMSO: F6.3

Michael Holford: D9.6, E1.4, page 126 top left, page 126 top left (inset), I2.3
Angelo Hornak: page 126 right
Inga Horwood: F1.3
Hutchison Library: B6.2a and b, B7.1, C3.1 D7.3, D9.1, E6.5, F7.5a, page 132 top right and bottom right, page 133 top left, page 136 top right, page 136 centre left
ICCE Photo Library: A1.2, A1.3, page 136 bottom right
Independent Television News Ltd: E4.6
ICI Mond Division: H4.2 bottom
Jodrell Bank: G9.3
Frank Lane Picture Agency Ltd: A2.5, B1.5, B1.8, B2.1a, B2.2a and b, B2.5, B7.2, B7.4, F10.2, F10.5, G2.1 right
Lead Development Association: page 132 bottom left
Lego UK Ltd: page 139
Lever Brothers: D8.4
Longman Group UK Ltd: A1.1, D3.3b
Lucas Film Ltd (Rex Features) I7.1
Mansell Collection: F4.1
MLURI Aberdeen: B3.4
Manchester City Council: D2.2
Medical Research Council, King's College: F4.5
Meteorological Office, Bracknell/S. Cornford: page 27
Meteorological Office, Bracknell: E1.2
Metra Non-Ferrous Metals Ltd: D3.2 top left
Microsense Systems Ltd: I7.6a
Keith Moseley: C5.3, G2.3, G2.6, G2.7, G4.7, G5.1, G8.1, G8.2, G8.3, G8.4, I3.4a and b
NASA: E2.3, G4.1 left
Mandy Nash: page 127 centre
National Coal Board: C6.1
National Maritime Museum: G7.5
Nuffield–Chelsea Curriculum Trust: D3.2 bottom left, D3.3c, D6.5 right, D7.5 top and bottom, D9.8a and b
Oxford Scientific Films: B1.7, D3.7, D9.5, D9.7a and b
Parkin Silversmiths Ltd: H5.4
Pilkington Electro Optic Materials Ltd: D6.6 top left
Pirelli General: page 133 top right
Polaroid: G1.1 centre
Popperfoto: F7.1
Derek Potter and Lynn Jarvis: page 8, page 42, page 43, page 44, D3.2 right, centre, and centre right, D3.3a, D3.4, D3.5, D3.6, D4.1a, D4.2a, b and c, D4.3a and b, D5.4, D6.5 left, D6.6 top right, D7.1, D7.2, D7.5 centre, D7.6, D8.3, D9.2, D9.3, H5.2, H5.5, I5.4
Press Association: I1.2
Rex Features: C2.5, C3.6, C6.5, E3.3, F6.4, F8.1, G2.1 centre, page 137 bottom right

Dr Bernard Richardson: G2.2
Dr Eric Robinson, Department of Geological Sciences, University College London: page 124 top left, top centre, top right, and bottom right
Ann Ronan Picture Library: C1.7, D6.1
The Royal Institution of Great Britain: I4.5
Royal Mail Stamps & Philately: I1.1
Science Museum: C4.4, C4.5
Science Photo Library: A2.2, A2.4, B1.2, C2.3, C6.2, C6.6, D5.5, D6.6 bottom left and bottom right, E3.1, E3.2, F1.1, F3.4, F4.3b, F4.4, F8.4, F10.1b, page 99, G1.2, G8.5, G9.1, G9.2, G9.5, G10.2, G10.3, G10.4, G10.5, G10.6, G10.7, page 125 top left, page 133 centre and bottom right, page 137 top left and bottom left, I2.4, I2.5, I3.2, I5.3, I7.3, I7.4, I7.5
Shell Photographic Library: D5.7
GR–Stein Refractories Ltd: page 125 bottom centre
Sterling Health: D8.5
Laurice Suess: page 132 top left
Telegraph Colour Library: E3.4b
Thorn Security: I7.6b
UKAEA: I7.2
G. Villermet, Institute of Ophthalmology: G6.8
Wind Energy Group: C1.2
W.H. Yoxall: E5.2, E6.6

From Beckett, B.S. *Illustrated human and social biology*. OUP, 1981: F8.7, G6.1, G6.2
Weather maps from *The Daily Telegraph*, 20 July 1988 and 21 July 1988: E2.2
The poem on page 26 is by Caroline Heath (aged 11) *Journal of biological education*, 17 (3) 1983.
From Hunt, J.A. and Sykes, A. *Chemistry* Longman, 1984: G9.4, H7.3, H7.4
From Lyth, M. (ed.) *Making patterns 1*. Exploring Science. Longman, 1985: E4.6
Weather maps drawn from data supplied by the Meteorological Office: E1.5, E4.1, E4.2
From ASE SATIS Unit 902: D8.9
From Van Helmont, J.B. *Ortus medicinae*. Amsterdam, 1668: F9.2

Thanks are also due to:
Clarissa who supplied the jewellery on page 127 bottom left (ear-rings)
Omega Electronics who supplied the equipment in figure I5.5
Tricia Rafferty who supplied the jewellery on page 127 bottom right (pin).

The Trust has made every effort to contact owners of illustrations appearing in this book. In the few instances where it has been unsuccessful it invites the copyright owners to contact it directly.